# Managing
# health and safety in
# **swimming pools**

**HSG179**

**HSE** BOOKS

This guidance is issued by the Health and Safety Commission.
Following the guidance is not compulsory and you are free to take
other action.  But if you do follow the guidance you will normally be
doing enough to comply with the law.  Health and safety inspectors
seek to secure compliance with the law and may refer to this guidance
as illustrating good practice.

*Managing health and safety in swimming pools* was prepared jointly by
the Health and Safety Commission and Sport England.
It is available from:

**Sport England Publications**
PO Box 255, Wetherby LS23 7LZ
Telephone: 0990 210255
Fax: 0990 210266

**HSE Books**
PO Box 1999, Sudbury, Suffolk CO10 6FS
Telephone: 01787 881165
Fax: 01787 313995

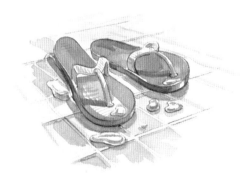

# Contents

Foreword  *iv*

Introduction  *viii*

General management of health and safety  4

The practicalities of managing health and safety  10

Physical environment  18

Supervision arrangements to safeguard pool users  54

General maintenance - plant and equipment  78

The pool water treatment system  88

Appendices  *106*

1    Membership of independent Working Group chaired by HSE  *108*

2    Safety signs  *109*

3    Swimming pool users' safety code  *110*

4    Pool Safety Operating Procedures (PSOP)  *111*

5    Hire of pool to outside organisations: check-list of points for inclusion in contracts  *112*

6    Scottish/National Vocational Qualifications (S/NVQs)  *113*

7    Addresses of relevant organisations  *114*

8    Dimensions for diving equipment  *117*

9    List of HSE and English Sports Council offices  *119*

10   References and further reading  *121*

     Index  *126*

# Foreword

Swimming is an important skill and healthy exercise for many thousands of adults and children. Sadly about 10-12 people drown in pools every year. Any drowning is a tragedy. Worse still, most drownings could have been prevented by better precautions by pool operators, greater care on the part of the bathers, or a combination of both.

However, swimming pools are far safer places to swim than open water, which claimed about 420 deaths in 1998. That is why the Health and Safety Commission (HSC) has traditionally taken a cautious approach to specifically regulating pool safety for fear of affecting the provision of public pools, and the numbers of adults and children who learn to swim in them. Instead we advocate reliance on the Health and Safety at Work etc Act 1974 and the supporting legislation and guidance to enforce safety.

The *Safety in swimming pools* guidance was first published in 1988. Since then technology, the law, and our general thinking on the management of health and safety have all moved on. This updated version of the guidance was, like its predecessor, drawn together using the expertise of a working group of representatives from private and public sectors, a local authority and professional bodies (for membership see Appendix 1). The group consulted widely and every effort was made to ensure that the views of all interested parties, including consumer groups and local authorities, were heard and reflected in the revised guidance. The wealth of the industry's experience and the practical approach of the Health and Safety Executive (HSE) contained in the guidance should be of use to all pool operators and in particular to those who are new to the responsibilities of pool management.

The decision by our two organisations to collaborate in taking the guidance forward to publication has enabled a wider range of expertise to be included, drawing particularly on Sport England's experience in design and management.

The main changes to this guidance are a general modernising of the document's style and content, and more comprehensive and practical advice on how to comply with existing legislation. It takes into account the technological advances in equipment used in the sector and new procedures which have become accepted as good industry practice. The content has also been broadened to include more specific topics such as design, manufacture, and operation of plant.

The aim of the new guidance is to build on the success of its predecessor by acting as a catalyst for continued improvements in health and safety standards. In line with the Commission's goal-setting approach, the guidance focuses on the need for pool operators to make provisions for health and safety based on risk, taking into account individual circumstances. It also emphasises the need for pool operators to take into consideration both pool users and employees when addressing the hazards associated with running a swimming pool.

Finally, although the guidance is addressed, first and foremost, to those who run pools, safety also depends on the care and good sense of bathers. This guidance also includes information about risks associated with bathing, and a suggested safety code for bathers to follow. Operators and managers are encouraged to bring this advice to the attention of pool users, particularly those who have charge of young children, or of organised groups.

**Frank Davies, CBE, OStJ**
Chairman, Health and
Safety Commission

**Trevor Brooking, CBE**
Acting Chairman
Sport England

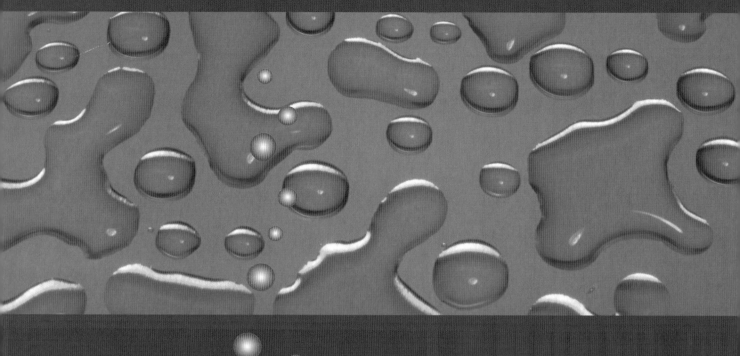

# Introduction

**1**    This booklet is a revision of the original guidance *Safety in swimming pools,* first published in 1988. The revision brings the guidance up to date with changes in health and safety law and new developments in relation to equipment, facilities and supervision arrangements.

### Who the guidance is for

**2**    The booklet provides guidance for those who have any involvement with the operation and management of health and safety in swimming pools; primarily pool owners (including local authority clients), pool operators (including management contractors), architects, engineers, designers, manufacturers and constructors. Aspects of this guidance will also apply to pool hirers. Its aim is to provide guidance on the risks associated with swimming pool operation and the precautions which may be taken to help achieve a safer environment for people who use swimming pools and employees who work at them.

**3**    The guidance refers to *pool operator* which should be regarded as a generic term to include anyone with a responsibility for health and safety in swimming pools.

### How the guidance should be used

**4** This guidance provides practical advice on how to comply with the law relating to the management of health and safety in swimming pools. Following the advice in the guidance will help you prevent or reduce accidents and incidence of ill health. You can refer to this guidance for management or technical information, and there is a section (starting with paragraph 314) which deals with the pool water treatment system.

### Pools to which the guidance applies

**5** The guidance applies to all types of pools (including paddling pools) used for swimming or leisure, except:

- pools designed for medical or therapeutic purposes (while in use for such purposes); and
- private swimming pools in domestic premises while being used solely by the owner, family and guests.

However, even in the case of these exceptions the guidance contains principles which, if followed, will promote a safer environment.

**6** The guidance has limited application to pools which consist of segregated areas of rivers, lakes or the sea. The booklet's recommendations on safe design, working methods and supervision should be followed insofar as they are relevant. In particular, attention should be paid to the signposting of hazards; supervision of equipment; adequacy of written procedures, including emergency procedures; and organisation and training of staff. Specific recommendations on training, etc, will, however, have limited application in pools with unclear water and irregular natural bottoms. Further information on the risks of open water is available (see Reference section[1,2]).

**7** The guidance applies to pool operators in pools completed and ready for use. It is also relevant to swimming pools that are in the process of being designed, constructed, refurbished, altered or improved.

### Risk assessment

**8** Risk assessment is central to the effective management of health and safety and features in several sections of this guidance. It is the duty of pool operators to ensure risks are adequately identified, assessed and controlled to prevent harm to employees or those affected by the work activity. Further information on how to do a risk assessment can be found in paragraphs 42-44.

### Meaning of 'reasonably practicable'

**9** The term 'so far as is reasonably practicable' appears often in this guidance and means that the degree of risk in a particular job or workplace needs to be balanced against the time, trouble, cost, benefit and physical difficulty of taking measures to avoid or reduce the risk. However, it should not be used as an excuse to avoid taking safety measures, and if unsure you should err on the side of caution.

### Status of advice

**10** Where you see the word '**must**' in this guidance it means a legal obligation, ie you are breaking the law if you do not comply. Terms such as '**should**' and, '**need to consider**' do not indicate a legal obligation, but do indicate good practice. There may be other legally acceptable ways of achieving the same objective. Other terms such as '**you may**', '**you are recommended to**' give general pointers on the way an objective may be met.

**11** There are references in this guidance to British, European or International Standards. You are not necessarily breaking the law if you do not conform to a relevant standard but you would be ignoring good advice. Where a relevant standard is more specific than this guidance or recommends a higher level of performance, you are advised to follow the standard.

### Subjects not covered in this guidance

**12** This guidance does not deal in detail with water quality or hygiene except insofar as these issues may also be covered under the Health and Safety at Work etc Act 1974. Details of where to find information on water quality and hygiene can be found in paragraphs 314-395 of this guidance. Fire precautions are not dealt with; policy responsibility on this issue lies with the Home Office and advice should be sought from the local fire authority.

### Enforcement of health and safety law

**13** Under the Health and Safety (Enforcing Authorities) Regulations 1998, the local authority is the enforcing authority for all pools unless it is the owner and/or occupier who has any extent of control of the activities or the equipment. HSE is the enforcing authority in pools occupied by local authorities, in educational establishments and at Ministry of Defence premises. Where there is doubt, seek clarification from the local HSE office (see Appendix 9 for a list of addresses).

### Further advice and information

**14** Further advice on many of the subjects mentioned in this guidance is available from the publications listed in the References and Further reading section. Advice can also be obtained from the home country Sports Councils (England, Scotland, Wales and Northern Ireland) on such issues as planning, design and management (see Appendix 9 for a list of addresses) or through the English Sports Council's *Facilities Factfile 1 - Recreation management*.[3] Advice on management and operational issues can also be obtained from the organisations listed in Appendix 9. HSE, or the relevant local authority, will be able to answer enquiries on the interpretation of health and safety law. Alternatively, you can also get further advice by phoning the HSE InfoLine on 0451 545500 (all calls charged at local rate).

# General management of health and safety

### What the law requires

**15** Every pool operator is responsible for health and safety. The Health and Safety at Work etc Act 1974, the Management of Health and Safety at Work Regulations 1992 and other similar legislation place general obligations on pool operators. Paragraphs 16-41 deal with the general legislation which all pool operators need to be aware of.

### Health and Safety at Work etc Act (HSW Act) 1974

**16** The Health and Safety at Work etc Act 1974 (HSW Act) places duties on employers, employees and self-employed people. It protects not only people at work, including those undertaking voluntary work, but also the general public who may be affected by work activities. Many of the requirements in this legislation are qualified with 'so far as is reasonably practicable' (see paragraph 9). The general requirements under the HSW Act are that equipment and plant are safe, the workplace is safe, there are safe systems of work and there is the provision of information, instruction, training and supervision needed to ensure that safety.

**17** Employees must do all that is reasonably practicable to take care of their own health and safety and that of others, including those undertaking voluntary work, who may be affected by their acts or omissions at work and they must co-operate with their employers in complying with statutory health and safety obligations. Manufacturers and those installing equipment have a duty under section 6 of this Act to ensure their products do not cause harm and are safe to use, including the provision of instructions on use and maintenance of equipment provided.

### Management of Health and Safety at Work Regulations (MHSWR) 1992

**18** As a pool operator, under the Management of Health and Safety at Work Regulations (MHSWR) 1992, you must carry out an assessment of the risks which may affect employees, and others, as a result of the work activity. These requirements also take into account members of the public using the pools. You will then need to take appropriate action to eliminate or reduce those risks as far as is reasonably practicable. The principles of risk assessment can be found in paragraphs 42-43.

**19** MHSWR 1992 also requires employers to:

- make arrangements for implementing the health and safety measures identified to reduce the risk;
- appoint competent people to help them implement the arrangements;
- set up emergency procedures;
- provide clear information and training to employees;
- establish procedures for employees to follow if a situation of serious or imminent danger were to arise;
- co-operate on health and safety matters with other employers who share the same workplace and co-ordinate an exchange of information about such matters; and
- consult with employees on health and safety matters.

### Workplace (Health, Safety and Welfare) Regulations (WHSWR) 1992

**20** The Workplace (Health, Safety and Welfare) Regulations (WHSWR) 1992 cover a wide range of basic health, safety and welfare issues and apply to most workplaces. The Regulations expand on the general duties under the HSW Act (see paragraphs 16-17).

**21** These Regulations cover subjects such as: temperature; ventilation; lighting; cleanliness and waste materials; room dimensions and space; maintenance; floors and traffic routes; toilet, washing, staff changing and clothes storage facilities; supply of fresh drinking water; and facilities for rest and eating meals.

### Provision and Use of Work Equipment Regulations (PUWER) 1998

**22** The Provision and Use of Work Equipment Regulations (PUWER) 1998 expand upon the general duties of the HSW Act and require that work equipment supplied to employees is suitable, used safely and properly maintained. Work equipment, regardless of its age, should not cause a risk to health and safety.

**23** PUWER makes more explicit the general duties already placed on employers, the self-employed and people in control to provide safe plant and equipment.

**(24)** Pool operators will need to ensure that:

- work equipment is suitable and properly maintained;
- their employees are properly informed about the work equipment including foreseeable abnormal situations which may arise during its operation; and
- their employees are competent in the use of work equipment.

### Construction (Design and Management) Regulations (CDM) 1994

**(25)** The Construction (Design and Management) Regulations (CDM) 1994 apply to construction projects (including, for example, refurbishment and demolition). The Regulations aim to improve the poor record of health and safety in construction by involving all those who can contribute to better management and design. There are a number of key duty holders: these are clients, designers, contractors, and a new function of 'planning supervisor'. The Regulations also introduce new documents - health and safety plans and the health and safety file - which involve all the duty holders, including the client.

**(26)** The CDM Regulations 1994 generally apply to construction work which is expected to last for more than 30 days (or involving more than 500 person-days) *or* which involves five people or more on site at any one time. However, regulation 13, which deals with design work, applies whenever design work is carried out for any construction project. Also, most of the Regulations apply if the work includes demolition or dismantling, as these activities are considered to create higher risks to health and safety.

### Electricity at Work Regulations 1989

**(27)** The Electricity at Work Regulations 1989 cover health and safety duties for the safe use of electricity at work. The Regulations require that electrical installations and equipment are properly constructed, maintained and fit for the purpose and environment in which they are used. This is particularly important in the humid or wet environments associated with swimming pools. For further details see paragraphs 294-313.

### Manual Handling Operations Regulations 1992

**(28)** Manual handling is the transporting or supporting of loads by hand or by bodily force.

**(29)** Pool operators will need to consider the risks from manual handling to the health and safety of their employees. If risks exist, the Manual Handling Operations Regulations 1992 apply, requiring all employers to:

- **avoid** the need for hazardous manual handling, as far as reasonably practicable;
- **assess** the risk of injury from any hazardous manual handling which cannot be avoided; and
- **reduce** the risk of injury from hazardous manual handling, as far as reasonably practicable.

**(30)** Pool operators are responsible for assessing and reducing risks from manual handling in the workplace. A basic precaution is to provide employees with basic training in handling techniques; however, you should also consider other more direct ways to reduce risk.

**31** Employees should:

- follow appropriate systems of work laid down for their safety;
- make proper use of equipment provided for their safety;
- co-operate with their employer on health and safety matters.

**32** When manual handling is unavoidable, review the task and think about how good techniques can help reduce the risk. This could include reorganisation or redesign of the task, sharing the load or using mechanical handling equipment.

### Control of Substances Hazardous to Health (COSHH) Regulations 1994

**33** As a pool operator you must carry out a COSHH assessment in order to protect your workforce and visitors against health risks from hazardous substances used at work. Having assessed the risks you will need to decide what precautions are necessary to prevent or control exposure. You will need to record and monitor the procedures and ensure that the control measures are used and maintained. You must also ensure that your employees are properly informed, trained and supervised (see paragraphs 317-343).

### Reporting of Injuries, Diseases and Dangerous Occurrences Regulations (RIDDOR) 1995

**34** Employers, the self-employed and people in control of premises where work is carried out, including pool operators, have duties under the Reporting of Injuries, Diseases and Dangerous Occurrences Regulations (RIDDOR) 1995. They must report certain work-related accidents and cases of ill health to the appropriate health and safety enforcing authority (see paragraph 13). Failure to do so is a criminal offence. For further details about reporting accidents, ill health or dangerous occurrences see paragraphs 54-57.

### Health and Safety (Safety Signs and Signals) Regulations 1996

**35** These Regulations require employers to provide specific signs whenever there is a risk that has not been avoided or controlled by other means, eg by safe systems of work. There is no need to provide a sign if it would not help to reduce the risk, or where the risk is not significant. Pool operators will need to take into account, as part of the risk assessment, provision of safety signs as an effective way to help control the risks, particularly in relation to the safe use of facilities by bathers. For further details see paragraphs 64-67.

### Diving at Work Regulations 1997

**36** The Diving at Work Regulations 1997 cover all dives when one or more divers undertake work activities. The Regulations apply to everyone, from the client, who commissions the work, to the diver undertaking the work. Everyone involved has a responsibility to ensure the health and safety of those taking part in the diving project. The Regulations seek to control, through risk assessment, the hazards and risks associated with diving. The employer has a responsibility, so far as is reasonably practicable, to plan and manage the work to protect the health and safety of everyone taking part.

**Employers' Liability (Compulsory Insurance) Act 1969**

(37) Pool operators are responsible for the health and safety of their employees while they are at work. Employees may be injured at work, or they or former employees may become ill as a result of their work. They may try to claim compensation from their employer if they believe the employer is responsible. The Employers' Liability (Compulsory Insurance) Act 1969 places a duty on employers to ensures that they have a minimum level of insurance cover against compensation claims for injury or disease of their employees arising out of their employment.

(38) Public liability insurance is different. It covers employers for claims made against them by members of the public, but not for claims made by employees. While public liability insurance is voluntary, employers' liability insurance is compulsory.

**Fire Precautions (Workplace) Regulations 1997**

(39) The Fire Precautions (Workplace) Regulations 1997 provide minimum fire safety standards in places where people work (including shared areas and facilities and the means of access to the workplace). Pool operators, like any other employer, have a duty to comply with them. Where you or another employer do not have control over parts of the workplace, there is a responsibility on the person who does (usually the owner or landlord) to make sure those parts comply with the Regulations.

**Health and Safety (Enforcing Authority) Regulations 1998**

(40) Health and Safety (Enforcing Authority) Regulations 1998 allocate enforcement responsibility for the Health and Safety at Work etc Act 1974, between HSE and local authorities. The Regulations will reduce dual enforcement in business (see paragraph 13).

**Confined Spaces Regulations 1997**

(41) These Regulations were made under the Health and Safety at Work etc Act (HSW Act) 1974 and came into force on 28 January 1998. The Regulations apply in all premises and work situations in Great Britain subject to the HSW Act, with the exception of diving operations and below ground in a mine (there is specific legislation dealing with confined spaces in these cases). These Regulations also extend outside Great Britain in a very limited number of cases.

# The practicalities
# of managing
# health and safety

### Principles of risk assessment

**42** An assessment of risk is nothing more than a careful examination of aspects of work that could cause harm to people, to establish whether enough precautions have been taken to prevent harm, or whether more precautions need to be taken. As part of the risk assessment, pool operators will need to consider all the hazards and risks associated with the pool.

- A **hazard** is anything that may cause harm.
- A **risk** is a chance, great or small, that someone will be harmed by a hazard.

**43** The aim is to make sure that no one gets hurt or becomes ill. There are five steps which pool operators need to take to make sure a proper risk assessment is done:

**Step 1    Look for the hazards**
You will need to look at what may cause harm to your employees, or other people, as a result of the work activity.

**Step 2    Decide who might be harmed, and how**
You will need to look at **who** may be affected by the work activity and **how** they may be affected; this may include members of the public, cleaners, visitors, contractors *working on the premises*, and maintenance personnel.

### Step 3    Assess the risks and take appropriate action

If you find a hazard which may be a risk to employees, or other people, you will need to decide what steps have to be taken to eliminate or reduce those risks as far as is reasonably practicable.  What needs to be done depends on whether the hazard is low risk or high risk.  You can determine this by looking at what type of harm or injury may arise and how often it may happen. It may be possible to remove the hazard altogether or to take steps to lower the risk to an acceptable level.  If there is no risk present, then you do not need to take any action.  Confirm that you have reduced risks as far as possible by checking your standards against published guidance such as relevant HSE publications.

### Step 4    Record the findings

If you have five or more employees in the organisation, you are required by law to record the significant findings from a risk assessment. This means you will need to write down the more significant hazards and record the most important conclusions. There is no need to show how the risk assessment was carried out, provided you can show that:

- a proper check was made;
- those who might be affected were consulted;
- all the obvious significant hazards were dealt with and account was taken of the number of people who could be involved;
- the precautions are reasonable and the remaining risk is low.

### Step 5    Review the assessment from time to time and revise it if necessary

It is important that you check the risk assessment from time to time, especially if there is a change in working procedures. You will need to ensure that the assessment takes into account new hazards which may cause harm to the health and safety of your employees, or other people who may be affected by the change in working conditions.

**44**  HSE's publication *5 steps to risk assessment*[4] gives further details on how do a risk assessment and can be obtained free from HSE Books (see Reference section).

### How to manage health and safety

**45**  As a pool operator you may be employed by a local authority or an organisation which has a corporate health and safety policy; you should ensure that you refer to it when setting your own policy.  However, the policy which you set will need to take account of local circumstances.

To effectively manage health and safety, pool operators may find it useful to follow the 'five steps to health and safety'.  These are as follows:

### Step 1    Set your policy

Your health and safety policy (see paragraph 46 on what to include in a health and safety policy) should influence all your activities, including the selection of people, equipment and materials, the way work is done and how you design and provide goods and services.  A written statement of your policy and the organisation and arrangements for implementing and monitoring it, demonstrate to your staff, and anyone else, that hazards have been identified and risks assessed, eliminated or controlled.

### Step 2    Organise your staff

To make your health and safety policy effective, you need to get your staff involved and committed to it. This can be achieved by assessing the skills of your staff and providing training and advisory support. You will need to allocate responsibilities and ensure that people understand their responsibilities. Staff and their representatives will need to be consulted and involved in planning and reviewing performance, writing procedures and solving problems. You will also need to communicate effectively with your staff by providing information about hazards, risks and preventative measures and regularly discussing health and safety. You will need to make your employees aware of the safety policy statement. If the statement is short, employees can be given individual copies or copies could be sent electronically. If this is not practicable, copies could be posted on notice-boards. The same distribution arrangements should then apply when the statement is revised.

### Step 3    Plan and set standards

Planning for health and safety involves setting objectives, identifying hazards, assessing risks and implementing standards of performance. You should put your plans in writing. Standards help to build a positive culture and control risks. They should identify who does what, when, and the result expected. Revision of the safety policy statement will need to take place as and when necessary. There are many reasons why a revision may be necessary, for example when new plant or new hazards are introduced to the workplace; organisational change; changes of personnel; or in light of experience, perhaps after monitoring. Depending on the extent of the revision, an amendment slip, an amended page or a whole revised statement may be issued.

### Step 4    Measure your performance

You will need to measure your health and safety performance. Active monitoring, before things go wrong, involves regular inspection and recording of the inspections and checking to ensure the standards are being implemented and management controls are working. Reactive monitoring, after things have gone wrong, involves learning from your mistakes. You need to ensure information from active and reactive monitoring is used to identify situations that create risks, and then do something about them.

### Step 5    Learn from experience: audit and review

Monitoring provides the information to enable you to review activities and decide how to improve performance. Audits complement monitoring activities by looking to see if your policy, organisation and systems are actually achieving the right results. Combine the results from measuring performance with information from audits to improve your approach to health and safety management. You will then need to review the effectiveness of your health and safety policy.

### What should be included in a safety policy statement?

If, as an organisation, you have five or more employees, you must, by law, have a written statement of your health and safety policy. The statement should set out your general policy for protecting the health and safety of your employees at work and should include the organisation and arrangements for putting that policy into practice. The length and complexity will vary according to the circumstances of the particular pool but should include safe operating procedures and an emergency action plan. The statement should include:

- the names of key individuals and their responsibilities for health and safety;
- a list of the hazards and the safe systems of work/precautions for avoiding them;
- arrangements for dealing with injury, fire and other emergencies;
- arrangements for providing the instruction, training and supervision to ensure that safe systems of work are always adopted and adhered to;
- arrangements to ensure that employees follow the rules and precautions.

Further information on writing a policy statement is available from HSE Books.

**Pool safety operating procedures for operation**

**47** A written Pool Safety Operating Procedure (PSOP) consists of the Normal Operating Plan (NOP) and the Emergency Action Plan (EAP) for the pool, changing facilities and associated plant and equipment. The plans can be kept as written documents or stored electronically, provided that staff have access to them and that they are available for inspection by your enforcing authority, if required.

**48** The NOP should set out the way a pool operates on a daily basis. It should include details of the layout, equipment, manner of use, user group characteristics and any hazards or activity-related risks.

**49** The EAP should give specific instructions on the action to be taken, by all staff, in the event of any emergency.

**50** Staff must not only be aware of the PSOP, the NOP and the EAP but should be instructed and trained to work in accordance with the provisions therein.

**51** Where a pool is hired by organisations, such as swimming clubs, the relevant sections of the plan must be made known to the organisation and, where necessary, training given and regular checks made to ensure compliance. Details of documentation, training provided and checks should be recorded (see Appendix 5 for more details).

**52** All parts of the PSOP should be regularly reviewed and revised if necessary, particularly with the installation of new equipment or after a major incident, eg an accident which requires hospitalisation of the injured person or a near-drowning. Staff and outside organisations should be made aware when a revision has taken place. A detailed check-list outlining the key features of both the NOP and the EAP is included at Appendix 4.

**53** Where the pool is an ancillary part of a larger complex (eg a hotel, hospital or school), a senior member of management should be clearly designated as responsible for safe pool operation.

**Reporting accidents**

**54** The reporting requirements are set out in the HSE free leaflet *Everyone's guide to RIDDOR*[5] and the more detailed *Guide to the Reporting of Injuries, Diseases and*

*Dangerous Occurrences Regulations 1995.*[6] If you are in any doubt as to whether an accident is reportable, you should contact your local authority or local HSE office, who will be able to advise you accordingly.

**55** The following information should give you a guide on what incidents are reportable. Under the Regulations, pool operators must:

- notify the enforcing authority without delay (eg by telephone), followed by a completed accident form (F2508) sent within ten days, if there is a work-related accident and:
  - an employee or a self-employed person working on the premises is killed or suffers a 'major' injury (including as a result of physical violence); or
  - a member of the public is killed or taken to hospital; or
  - there is a 'dangerous occurrence' as defined in the Regulations;
- send a completed accident report form (F2508) to the enforcing authority within ten days if there is a work-related accident and an employee or self-employed person does not suffer a 'major' injury but is unable to do their normal work for more than three days (including as a result of physical violence);
- send a completed disease report form (F2508a) to the enforcing authority as soon as they receive notification from a doctor that an employee is suffering from one of the work-related diseases set out in RIDDOR.

---

Examples of reportable incidents include:

- Pool user slips on a wet floor and is taken to hospital.
- Lifeguard is injured as a result of violence by another person.

---

**56** 'Major injury' is defined in RIDDOR and includes injuries such as: certain fractures and dislocations; unconsciousness; admittance to hospital for more than 24 hours; and acute illness caused by absorption of any substance. 'Dangerous occurrences' are serious accidents which do not lead to a reportable injury. They include the failure of lifts and lifting equipment; electrical short circuit or overload causing fire or explosion; and the release of any substance with the potential to damage health.

**57** Pool operators may find it a useful practice to record and monitor all accidents and incidents, particularly successful rescues. This will help:

- to ensure effective risk assessment;
- to identify possible problem areas; and
- in possible cases of civil legal action at a later date.

**Providing first aid**

**58** The MHSWR 1992 require employers to assess risks to the health and safety both of employees and of persons not employed by them, including members of the public, in order to identify the measures they need to take to comply with any health and safety requirements, and to make arrangements to ensure these measures are effectively managed. Health and safety requirements in respect of employees are often specified in regulations - for example the Health and Safety

(First Aid) Regulations 1981 place a requirement on employers to provide first aid for their employees while they are at work. Requirements in respect of other people are covered by the general duty in section 3 of the HSW Act 1974 to ensure the health and safety of non-employees.

**59** Pool operators will need to decide, as part of the risk assessment, the first-aid provision needed. Consideration needs to be given to:

- the needs of staff;
- the type, quantity and location of equipment;
- the numbers of suitably qualified staff.

**60** Pool operators have a duty towards those using their pool, therefore it is strongly recommended that **the needs of the pool users are considered** as part of the risk assessment in relation to first-aid provision.

**61** Specialised first-aid equipment and personal protective equipment (PPE) should be properly stored. Specialised equipment will need to be stored near the first-aid box while PPE will need to be stored close to where it is required. The equipment will need to be regularly checked to ensure it remains in good condition.

**62** Lifeguards usually prefer to use a face mask to separate themselves from direct contact with the casualty when carrying out expired air resuscitation. All lifeguards should be trained in the use of such face masks. The air supplied to casualties can be enriched by the supply of oxygen through suitable face masks. This increases the prospects of successful resuscitation and is also a useful way of reducing risk of infection.

**63** Apart from face masks and oxygen insufflation devices, it is recommended that mechanical resuscitation equipment should not be kept at the poolside. Mechanical resuscitation equipment should only be used by trained paramedic or medical staff.

**Safety signs**

**64** The Health and Safety (Safety Signs and Signals) Regulations 1996 cover prohibition, mandatory warning and emergency escape or first-aid signs. Acoustic signals are also safety signs under these Regulations and may be needed, for example, with wave machines.

**65** Prohibition signs (as used for 'no diving') should be a white circle with red edging and diagonal line. The warning signs need to be triangular with black edging and a yellow background, and should contain a black pictogram indicating the danger. Examples of suitable signs are contained in the Regulations, including the pictogram for general danger which consists of a large exclamation mark. Pool operators are free to design or choose suitable pictograms, including the use of composite signs, which will help maintain a safe pool environment. Signs may be particularly important where:

- there are any sudden changes in depth and it is necessary to clearly mark the depth of water, especially at shallow and deep ends;

- it is necessary to show areas where it is unsafe to swim, or to dive (and indicating any sudden changes in depth which could pose a hazard);
- there are slippery surfaces;
- it is necessary to provide instructions on the safe use of the pool and its equipment.

**66** Pool operators will need to:

- maintain any safety sign which is provided;
- ensure that signs are located in appropriate positions and unobstructed, eg by equipment/plant, etc;
- explain the signs to their employees, and tell them what they need to do when they see a safety sign, particularly in relation to bathers;
- maintain the depth of water in accordance with the information displayed.

**67** Leading sign-makers will stock a selection of signs, including safety signs. See Appendix 2 for examples of suitable signs to use in swimming pools.

# Physical environment

## Introduction

The effective management of health and safety in any swimming pool starts with careful design.
All of those involved in designing new pools or upgrading existing ones will need to give the highest priority to ensuring that they provide bathers and staff with a facility that is safe. Three requirements need to be met in order to achieve this:

- the layout of the pool hall, and the pool tank (including its dimensions, profile and any water features), should be designed so as to make the safe use and supervision of the pool easy to achieve without complex or costly management arrangements;
- the layout of the ancillary areas, including the changing, clothes storage, shower and toilet areas, should be similarly designed for safe use;
- the structural elements, materials, finishes and details which are used in the construction of these areas, including the pool hall enclosure, tank and equipment, and the way they are assembled should be those which are most appropriate to achieving a safe-to-use physical environment.

There are specific sources of information from which the technical design and planning standards that are recommended in the design of swimming pools can be obtained. Everyone who is involved in the process of specifying, designing and constructing pools should be familiar with these design and planning standards and should ensure that they are given careful consideration in all pool projects. The main sources of published technical guidance are available in the Reference and Further reading sections.

70  It is not the purpose of this guide to repeat all of the technical advice outlined in paragraph 69. But it is important to draw the attention of all of those involved in the design process to the implications of their work for the pool operator. What might be thought a small change in the layout of the pool or in the finishes specified could have a significant impact on the ability of the pool to be used safely. If that change is ill-considered and creates a serious design flaw, the result might be an increase in accidents. More likely it will be an increase in the cost of operating the pool (perhaps through the employment of additional staff) in order to compensate for the resulting problems.

71  One way of anticipating the management consequences of design decisions is to include an experienced facility manager on the design team. Although it may not be possible to include the person who will ultimately manage the facility, it should not be too difficult to obtain the services of someone from within the client organisation, or who is managing a similar facility elsewhere, to give advice and guidance during the various development stages of the project.

72  Where a new pool is being designed or major improvements/additions are being made to an existing pool, the main factors affecting safety which should be considered are set out in paragraphs 73-130 and Table 1. It must be reiterated that the technical documents referred to in paragraph 69 will provide a greater level of detail, and should be referred to directly.

**Pool tank**

*Pool tank profile*

73  It is recommend that all pool profiles are based on a number of important safety principles:

- abrupt changes in depth should be avoided in water less than 1.5 m in depth;
- steep gradients should be avoided - a maximum gradient of 1 in 15 is recommended for water depths up to 1.5 m;
- changes in depth should be clearly identified by the use of colour-contrasted materials or patterned finishes so as to indicate to bathers when they are proceeding to water of a different depth. Where colour is used, this should not reduce the visibility of a body lying on the pool bottom;
- a minimum water depth of 1 m is recommended for larger pools used for training and/or competition. For small community pools without a separate learner pool, a depth of 900 mm is recommended because this is more appropriate to young children and for teaching purposes.

74  The introduction of a movable floor(s)/bulkhead(s) will affect the pool tank profile and will create a wider range of different profiles. Care should be taken to ensure no additional hazards are created. The overall profile should still meet the above principles and where this is impractical, or cannot be achieved, options for controlling any potential hazards need to be considered.

*Pool tank edge*

**75** The pool tank edge should be colour-contrasted with the pool water so as to render it clearly visible to bathers in the water and on the pool surround. This is particularly important for deck-level pools where the pool edge may be partially submerged.

**76** Fixed raised pool ends are recommended for main pools with deck-level edge channels, where a pool is used predominantly for training and/or racing. The raised ends help the swimmer to easily identify the end walls of the tank.

**77** In a leisure pool where the pool tank bottom slopes gently from a beach area to deeper water, there is no need to highlight the water's edge providing there are no 'upstands' or steps between the pool and its surrounds.

*Pool tank detailing*

**78** It is recommended that the detailed design of the pool tank should ensure that:

- the pool tank should have no sharp edges or projections that could cause injury to bathers, especially below the water level. Careful consideration will need to be given to the design of recesses, ledges, or rails so as to ensure that they are not a hazard;
- wave machine openings, sumps, or inlets and outlets of the pool water circulation system should have suitable protective covers or grilles. They should be designed to prevent limbs and fingers getting trapped. Undue suction should not be created, which could result in a body being held against a grille, and there should be no exposed sharp edges. This is particularly important in areas of moving water;
- there should be at least two outlets per suction line at a sufficient distance apart to prevent a body being drawn or trapped by two suction line outlets. The amount of suction produced at any single outlet position should not be sufficient to result in a body being drawn towards it and held in position or entangle hair;
- where handrails are provided, they should be recessed into the pool tank in such a way that it is not possible for limbs to become trapped between the grab-rail and the rear wall of the recess or the tank wall;
- if a resting ledge is to be provided this should be recessed into the pool wall. If, for some reason, this is not possible, the ledge should be colour-contrasted and warning signs displayed to alert bathers, who are entering the water, to its presence.

*Pool tank bottom*

**79** A slip-resistant and non-abrasive finish should be provided in the following areas:

- on the end walls of the pool as a turning pad to aid tumble turns or for swimmers starting backstroke events;
- in leisure pools on the beach area and other shallow water areas where bathers may become unbalanced when a wave machine or other feature is operating.

**80** If racing lines are not to be included then a line running along the centre of the pool will assist bathers to determine sudden changes in water depth. The ability to see the bottom of the pool clearly is essential to effective lifeguarding. Pool floor patterns which would make it more difficult to recognise a body at the bottom of the pool should not be used.

**Access to the pool and the pool hall**

*Circulation in 'wet' areas and around the pool*

**81** Abrupt changes in floor level, including steps, should be avoided in 'wet' areas wherever possible, including changing rooms, shower areas, toilets and on the pool surround.

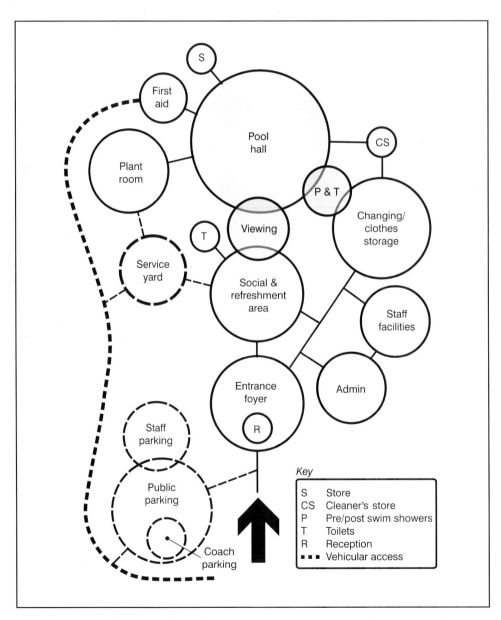

**Figure 1**  Good planning and circulation can ease management problems and enhance safety. This diagram illustrates a suggested relationship between the main areas of the building. Note particularly that:
   i)    access from the changing/pre-cleanse area should preferably not be at a point on the pool surround adjacent to deep water;
   ii)   storage areas for chemicals should be away from 'public' areas and accessible directly from outside.

**82** Access to the pool hall from changing rooms or pre-swim shower areas should present the bather with water less than 1.2 m in depth. Other features which affect design, such as the location of access stairs to water slides, should avoid the possibility of bathers queuing near deeper water without a protective barrier. Ramps may be provided to give people with disabilities easier access to the pool. If a ramp is provided in a main pool, it should not protrude into the bathing/swimming area.

**83** Where a freeboard rises substantially above 380 mm, consideration should be given to the need for a protective barrier at the pool edge.

**84** The pool surrounds and other circulation areas should be designed so as to ensure the free flow of bathers and the avoidance of congestion. A minimum surround width of 2 m is recommended, but it may be possible for a narrower width to be used safely in some circumstances. The required width should be determined by reference to:

- how the pool will be used - for instance, whether it will be used for training or competition;
- where people will circulate, taking into consideration entry/exit from changing areas and the pool tank, queues for water features, fire escapes and any other areas where there is the potential for congestion. In addition, pool operators need to consider what the maximum number of bathers using the pool surround is likely to be at any one time; this should also take into account use by people in wheelchairs.

*Access to the pool tank*

**85** Access to a pool tank may be provided by built-in steps or ladders according to the type of pool. These should provide easy and safe entry to, and exit from, the water. Fewer entry points may be needed where the pool edge is of deck-level type since many bathers find it easier to enter and leave this type of pool directly from the poolside.

**86** Entry steps and ladders should not interfere with the use of the pool for competition or training and should be recessed so as not to disrupt or endanger swimmers. The most appropriate arrangements for access are suggested as follows:

- for main pools, by means of a recessed ladder at each end of the pool tank in each side wall, approximately 1 m from the pool tank end wall. Additional steps at the mid-point of the tank could also be considered;
- for learner pools, by means of steps running along part of the pool. In irregular-shaped pools these can be designed to follow the shape of the tank. Intermediate handrails should be provided;
- for leisure pools with high freeboards, recessed steps allowing entry and exit from all water areas should normally be located not more than 15 m apart;
- for splashdown pools, the exit steps should be at the opposite end to the slide exit point.

## Design of steps and ladders

(87) Handrails, steps and ladders providing access to the pool:

- must be of sufficient strength and firmly fixed to the surround and tank walls;
- should be designed to ensure that finger, limb and head traps are not created, either between the treads or the tank walls, or between the grab-rails and the tank walls;
- should be designed with their likely user in mind. Steps providing access to learner pools or shallow water should have a shallow riser (between 150 mm and 160 mm) and be wide enough (300 mm minimum) to allow easy use by children or an adult carrying a child. The leading edge of each step should be colour-contrasted for increased visibility from both in and out of the water;
- should have treads which are slip-resistant and have no sharp edges;
- should be designed giving consideration to the ease of access to and exit from the pool by users with restricted mobility or those with disabilities.

## Design of ramps

(88) Ramps providing access to the pool:

- should have a gradient that does not exceed 1 in 15;
- should have a clear width of 1 m;
- should have a slip-resistant surface;
- should have handrails on both sides of the ramp;
- should have sufficient space at the bottom and top of the ramp for manoeuvring a wheelchair;
- should not, if provided in a main pool, protrude into the competitive area.

## Floors and finishes

### Slip resistance

(89) Slip and trip hazards can be reduced by good design. Surface roughness, moisture displacement, the profile and surface pattern of the finish and foot-grip, all affect slip resistance. The slip resistance of any given surface will diminish if the gradient becomes steeper than 1 in 30 or is less than 1 in 60 (because such a shallow gradient is not sufficient to ensure that moisture drains away). Where falls outside the recommended range have to be specified, finishes should have a particularly high slip resistance. Floor finishes with different slip-resistance characteristics should not normally be specified in the same area.

(90) The normal recommended range for the fall in wet areas is between 1 in 35 and 1 in 60. When combined with a slip-resistant finish such as a '25-stud' ceramic tile, this should create a satisfactory surface.

### Movement joints

(91) Where movement joints are provided in order to meet the requirements of BS 5385: Part 3 1989 (amended 1992),[7] the compound used should be as hard as possible so as to reduce the likelihood that it can be pulled out of the joint.

### Drainage gullies

**92** Floor gullies, gutters and valleys should not constitute a tripping hazard, and the drainage outlet should have no sharp edges. They should also be easy to maintain and clean.

## Walls

### Finishes

**93** Wall finishes to circulation areas should be smooth for a height of 2 m minimum so as not to present a hazard to bathers moving around. Any projecting piers or columns should be provided with a rounded or bull-nosed edge. Consideration should be given to the safety implications of rocks, planting features and structures provided close to walkways.

## Glazing

**94** It is essential that any glazing used in the pool area is of the appropriate specification to ensure that it can withstand body impact (BS 6262: Part 4 1994).[8] If the pool is used, for example for water polo, windows will need protection against ball impact, for instance through the use of impact-resistant toughened glass or polycarbonate sheeting or netting. Consideration will need to be given to ways of reducing the amount of glare caused by the glazing which could affect the view of lifeguards and pool users.

## Ceilings

**95** The constructional design of ceilings and the roof deck over 'wet' areas should take into account the need to avoid condensation, which can affect the structural integrity of the roof itself. Detailed guidance on this issue can be found in the *Handbook of sports and recreational building design*[9] (available from Sport England Publications) and is also available from the Advisory Service of the Building Research Establishment. Suspended ceilings should be avoided wherever possible, but if they are essential they should be designed in such a way that allows routine inspection of the ceiling void, internal roof structure and light fittings.

## Specialised pool design elements

**96** Many swimming pools contain a number of features which present their own particular requirements to ensure safe operation. The design of such features should ensure that the pool operator has the least possible difficulty in achieving a safe operating environment.

**97** The detailed design issues related to these features are covered by the *Handbook of sports and recreational building design*,[9] to which all designers should refer. The key issues for safe design are highlighted in paragraphs 98-125.

### Diving

**98** As a general principle, when new pools are being designed, diving stages and springboards should only be installed over a separate purpose-designed pool.

This is to eliminate the risk of collision between swimmers and divers, and to reduce the hazards of deep water and the misuse of equipment. These hazards can easily be avoided by separation of the activities. The exception to this principle would be when a new pool is provided with a movable floor and bulkhead so that part of the pool tank can be altered to create a safe water depth for diving or swimming, and the bulkhead used as a physical barrier to separate the various activities.

**99** Facilities for competitive diving should comply with the dimensional standards which are based upon the guidance produced by FINA, the world swimming governing body. The specification produced by FINA is contained in Appendix 8. It should be noted that this is the specification current at the time of publication, and reference should always be made to the latest available information. These standards are also adequate for recreational diving.

**100** For both competitive and training purposes it is recommended that the surface of the water of the pool should be broken so that it is easily visible to the diver. This can be achieved either by an overhead spray positioned at the edge of the pool tank or, preferably, by a stream of air released from spurge units or air nozzle outlets cast into the pool bottom, which will cause ripples on the surface of the water. This also acts as a safety cushion for divers when training.

### Diving platforms and boards

**101** Diving boards, stages or platforms will need to be:

- of sound construction and adequate strength;
- adequately protected against corrosion;
- non-abrasive with a slip-resistant surface for divers to walk on; and
- safe to use - platforms more than 2 m above the poolside should have a suitable guard and mid-rails to prevent users falling from the open sides, but these barriers should not obstruct the view which lifeguards have of the platform. The barriers should be designed in accordance with FINA regulations; they should be continuous and the only openings should be at the point of access and exit above the pool tank. The steps from the pool tank should be positioned to encourage divers to follow a safe exit route after completing their dives.

### Poolside starting blocks

**102** Poolside starting blocks provided for competition use can be removable or integrated with the pool structure and should preferably be located at the deeper end of the pool. Integral blocks may be preferred by some operators because of the inconvenience of fitting and removing temporary blocks. However, unskilled bathers risk serious injury by diving from starting platforms. It is therefore recommended that permanent blocks should not be provided in new pools. Management precautions should be taken to prevent the use of starting blocks by casual bathers during unprogrammed sessions.

**103** Raised pool ends (300 mm and above) to which starting blocks can be fixed are recommended for deck-level pools which are used primarily for training and competitions, and should be provided at both ends of the pool.

## Water slides

The following advice applies to slides that are 2 m or over in height above the point of entry to the water and discharge into the pool tank. Some of these principles will also apply to smaller slides and pools used by children.

- The design of the slide, including the splashdown area, should meet the guidelines set out in the latest European Standard BSEN 1069: Part 1 1996 entitled *Water slides over 2 m in height*.[10]
- The design of the slide should consider carefully the need for users to be 'managed' in their access to and use of the slide. This should be made as easy as possible for the pool operator, paying particular attention to where and how users will queue; the position of the lifeguard observation points; and how pool operators can control the slide's use (eg by the use of gates, etc).
- The design of the slide should minimise the need to have supports in circulation areas or where they obscure the view of lifeguards.
- Water slides should terminate into either a separate splashdown pool or a catch unit, which is a water-filled channel built as part of the slide. These should be carefully designed to ensure that bathers enter safely and can exit quickly.

The safety implications of water slides should be considered very carefully as some design features may disorientate or distract the user.

## Wave machines

The design of the wave formation and of the pool tank should be considered together to minimise the risk to bathers from being thrown against fixed parts of the structure by the motion of waves.

Although the height of the wave generated will vary with the type of equipment installed, the height of the freeboard will be higher than is found in a conventional pool. This may make it difficult for bathers to leave the pool. In such circumstances it is recommended that a recessed handgrip or ledge be provided at water level around the pool perimeter to the sides of the wave machine chamber, and where the freeboard exceeds 380 mm.

Access to the wave machine chamber should be suitably guarded to prevent bathers from entering the chamber. The method of guarding should take into consideration the possibility of entrapment of limbs.

All motors, shafts, gears, pulleys, chains, sprockets and similar moving parts employed for the production of waves should be enclosed by guards, which must be kept in position at all times when the machinery is in motion, in accordance with BS 5304:1988.[11]

## Movable floors and bulkheads

The design of a movable floor and/or bulkhead, either for a new pool or for an existing pool, will need to include careful consideration of health and safety issues. The provision of a bulkhead or movable floor should not hinder circulation of water within the pool and should allow adequate mixing to take place.

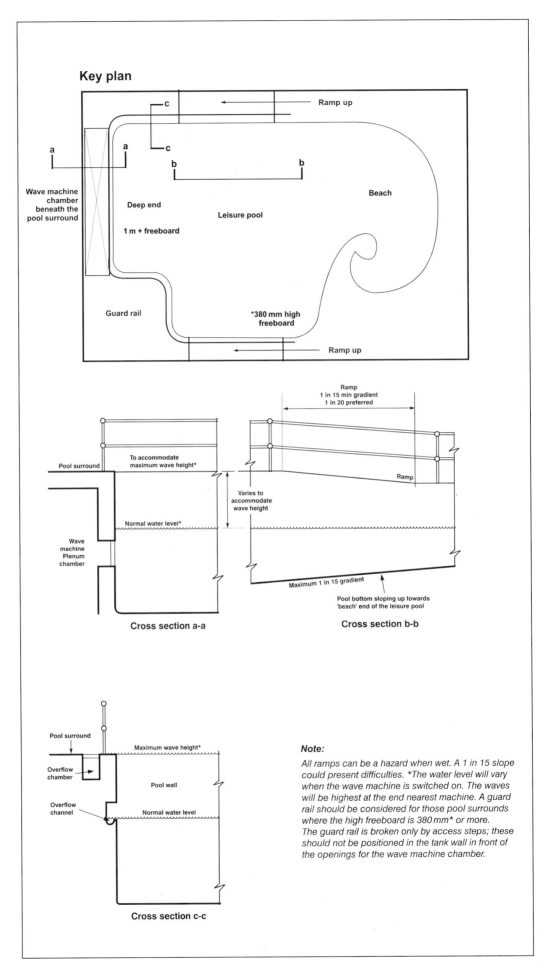

**Figure 2** Wave machines

*Movable floors*

**110** Movable floors which cover only part of the pool bottom should incorporate effective measures to ensure that bathers cannot gain access to the underside of the floor when it is in a raised position. This may be achieved by the use of a hinged flap or a submersible or laterally moving bulkhead which mates with the movable floor and the pool tank bottom.

**111** If a flap is used then the gradient of the flap when the floor itself is raised may be very steep. Precautions should be taken to prevent bathers from slipping off the flap. A dark-coloured line 100 mm wide should indicate where the platform finishes and the ramp starts. In many cases the only acceptable solution will be to prevent bathers from attempting to move to the edge of the floor. To effect this , a highly visible lane rope should be positioned between 500 mm and 1 m from the beginning of the flap, or alternatively, a bulkhead with a movable 'skirt' can be used to prevent access. Depending on the water depth, there may be a tripping hazard where the flap meets the pool bottom. The floor manufacturer should be consulted on what precautions, if any, are needed to overcome this problem.

**112** Care should be taken to ensure that there are no entrapment hazards around the edge of the floor. Flexible rubber gaskets may be used to fill the gaps which should not exceed 8 mm.

**113** If the floor is to be used in a tilted position to create a 'beach' effect, the gradient should not be more than 1 in 15 and the floor should be provided with a slip-resistant and non-abrasive surface.

**114** The control panel used to operate the floor should be located so that the operator has a clear view of the floor.

**115** Water depth indicators should be wall-mounted in a prominent position so that they can be seen easily by bathers, both in the pool and from the surround. The indicators should be clear and accurate. This is particularly important when the pool is used for diving. Where the floor is tilted for public use, an indicator should be wall-mounted close to each end of the floor indicating the depth of the water, whatever the position of the floor.

**116** If diving is one of the activities to be accommodated in the pool, the following points should also be taken into account:

- electrically-operated 'no diving' signs should be provided in the statutory format which should be clearly visible whenever the floor is in its swimming mode and a manual backup should always be available;

- diving facilities should not be accessible to bathers unless the floor is at its full diving depth. Various measures are possible to ensure that this condition is observed, and the floor manufacturer should be consulted on those which are most suitable for any given location.

*Bulkheads*

117    There are various types of bulkhead that may be provided to subdivide a pool so that different activities can be accommodated.  The bulkhead design should meet the following safety requirements:

- The space beneath the bottom of a laterally moving bulkhead is an area in which a bather might be hidden from the view of staff.  In a pool of constant depth, this hazard could be avoided through the fitting of a fixed infill panel or skirt between the base of the bulkhead and the pool bottom.  In pools where the bottom of the pool varies in depth, a flexible 'skirt' could be used.
- Warning notices prohibiting swimming beneath the bulkhead should be integrated into the design of the bulkhead and displayed on the poolside where they can be seen by bathers.
- Openings in the bulkhead below the waterline should not cause finger or limb traps.  Above the waterline, openings should not be wider than 100 mm.
- The underside of the bulkhead should be sealed to prevent a bather from getting trapped inside.
- The top surface of the bulkhead should be slip resistant and allow for the drainage of surface water.  Access panels should have a slip-resistant finish and be flush with the surface of the bulkhead.
- Where the bulkhead mates with the pool tank walls, the gap between the wall and the edge of the bulkhead should not cause finger or limb traps.
- Anchor connectors for lane ropes should not protrude beyond the face of the bulkhead.
- A recessed handgrip should be provided on each side of the bulkhead.
- When a submersible bulkhead is in a raised position, it should be mechanically secured or locked into the pool tank wall.  This should allow it to be unevenly loaded without causing a hazard.  If the bulkhead is installed in a leisure pool with wave-making facilities, the movement of the waves should not destabilise or create undue movement of the bulkhead or floor, where it is used in conjunction with a movable floor.
- Where a bulkhead is combined with a movable floor, the design should incorporate measures to prevent bathers from moving from shallow water created with the floor in the raised position to deep water on the other side of the bulkhead.  A removable barrier rail fixed to the top of the bulkhead would be one solution.
- Where the top of the bulkhead is at water level, the edge should be highlighted to make it visible to bathers.
- If a fixed bulkhead is to be constructed in the shallow end of an existing pool, it may be necessary to remodel the pool tank bottom on either side to create the appropriate water depths.

**Special features**

*Inner-tube rides*

118    Where ride enhancement devices in the form of rubber tubes/rings are used, rides should be designed to ensure that there is an adequate depth of water to prevent users from striking the bottom of any intermediate pools and also the splashdown pool. If the intermediate pool is designed to produce a whirlpool effect then consideration should be given to the use of ropes attached to the walls to allow

users to steady their motion and achieve forward movement. In addition life guards should have easy access to intermediate bowls/pools without having to travel down the body of the slide.

### Slow and fast river rides

Slow and fast rivers are a flat circuitous stream of water moved by booster pumps in which bathers float or swim and should be designed to:

- minimise the possibility of rider impact with walls and steps on entry and exit;
- make lifeguarding easy by providing appropriate lifeguarding stations from which the path of the river can be observed;
- make the checking of fixtures and fixings easy;
- allow riders to leave the stream of water easily, and exit into water no deeper than 1.2 m; and
- produce the minimum of undertow within the stream of water.

### Falling rapids

Falling rapids involve riders descending an inclined channel in a fast-flowing stream of water. There may be intermediate pools and/or weirs at the start of the separate sections of the channel.

Falling rapids are usually of a challenging nature and need to be restricted to confident swimmers. Designers will need to consider:

- the need to give prospective riders warning of the challenging nature of the ride and the restrictions which they will need to observe when using it;
- control of the entry point and of the flow of bathers in each section so as to reduce the possibility of congestion and collision;
- the illumination of turbulent areas to highlight the presence of a submerged rider who may be in difficulty;
- ways to allow riders to leave the stream of water easily;
- the provision of ropes or handholds to enable riders to manoeuvre themselves over weirs;
- the provision of lifeguarding stations which will enable lifeguards to view the whole length of the ride and allow the lifeguards to enter the water in the event of an emergency, or to assist a user in leaving the feature;
- the means by which an injured and possibly unconscious person can be removed from the ride;
- the means by which water flow can be cut off in an emergency without endangering users; and
- if any part of the ride is located outdoors, the need to provide shelter for lifeguards from adverse weather conditions, such as direct sunlight or rain.

### Spas

Although they are often operated as an-add on feature within a pool hall, spa pools cannot be considered simply as mini swimming pools. The designer of any pool environment in which a spa is proposed should consider the inclusion of an alarm adjacent to the spa so that the attention of pool staff can be drawn quickly to any emergency. Particular attention should be given to ensure users are not harmed by the water/air flow inlets and that body parts or hair are not caught by suction outlets.

**123** It is operationally difficult to see below the water surface in spas, so steps leading into the spa should have colour-contrasted nosing (rounded edges) and accompanying handrails. Underwater lighting is also a useful way of highlighting seats and steps.

### Pool hoists for the disabled

**124** Appropriate and suitable methods must be provided, by which those with a disability can gain access to the pool, either with or without assistance. The provision of mobile and fixed electrical/mechanical hoists can reduce substantially the amount of manual handling which will be necessary to assist those with a disability to gain access to the pool. Their provision should be considered in consultation with current or potential disabled users and/or organisations.

**125** The location of the hoists will need to be considered carefully to ensure that they are of maximum benefit, and do not represent an obstruction to the free movement of bathers and staff. Further advice can be obtained from the disability organisations listed in Appendix 7.

### Storage of equipment

**126** Equipment stored on the poolside is potentially hazardous, and designers should consider ways to ensure that there is sufficient separate storage accommodation and/or the pool surround width is sufficient to accommodate the equipment without obstructing the free movement of bathers and staff.

### Storage lockers

**127** Clothes lockers may be located throughout the changing area(s) or concentrated in a locker area. Any aisles which are created through the placement of lockers should be at least 1.2 m wide to allow for safe circulation and preferably 1.5 m wide.

**128** Keys and other sharp edges on locker doors may be a hazard to users. Doors should not hang open in such a way that someone using a lower locker could hit their head on the open door of an upper locker, therefore self-closing doors should preferably be used. However, strong spring-loaded doors can be a potential problem and are unpopular with users as they have to use a bare arm to hold them open while loading or unloading the locker.

### Managing design problems

**129** While good design will eliminate many potential hazards, most pool operators will have responsibility for an existing pool, in circumstances where they cannot make changes to its layout or major features. In such circumstances there may be minor changes or management measures that can be taken which would enable the pool to be used safely. New pools should not need such measures because good design will avoid the need for them.

130 Pools which are being improved or refurbished may contain hazards that are impossible to eradicate and therefore measures will need to be considered to ensure that they are safe to use. Table 1 identifies some of the design problems that may be found in an existing pool, and describes some of the management action that may be taken to solve them, depending on the outcome of a risk assessment. It is not intended to be comprehensive, nor will the measures described be appropriate for every situation. It is the responsibility of the pool operator to determine whether such management measures are a sufficient response to the hazards and risks identified.

**Table 1**   Identifying design problems and hazards that may be found in existing pools (see page 34)

*Notes to Table 1*

*Before deciding which option(s) for control is the most appropriate, it is recommended that the accident records are evaluated as these should give an indication of the order of priority for dealing with a specific problem.*

*With design problems that cannot be eliminated, the problem should be clearly identified in the Pool Safety Operating Procedure and by thorough and continual staff training. In addition, continuous checking and maintenance routines may help with some potential design problems.*

*For information on signs, refer to Appendix 2.*

**Table 1**    Identifying design problems and hazards that may be found in existing pools

| Identify design problem and hazards which may arise | Examine design problem - examples of checks which can be made | Examples of options for control |
|---|---|---|
| **1 Circulation** | | |
| **1.1 Access to the pool hall is located close to water deeper than 1.2 m**<br><br>Bathers may enter the water at the first entry point without checking that the water depth is appropriate - a particular problem for children and inexperienced swimmers | ● Check width of pool surround at point of entry | 1 If the pool surround is narrow at the point of entry (ie less than 2 m), provide warning signs that are clearly visible to bathers at the entry point to the pool hall and also within the changing areas<br><br>2 Locate staff so that they have a clear view of bathers entering the pool hall and can easily reach the water area at that point<br><br>3 If space is available, channel bathers to a safe water depth by means of physical barriers such as guard rail or planting features. The extent of the guard-rail and its positioning in relation to the pool edge may vary depending upon the pool edge profile, width of surround and pool tank configuration. Ideally, the guard-rail should be set back from the pool edge to allow staff access to the water area in front of the rail |
| **1.2 Routes within the pool hall to any water features require bathers to pass or queue near deep water**<br><br>Bathers may re-enter the pool inadvertently in deep water without checking the depth<br><br>Bathers may fall or be pushed into deep water - a particular problem may occur as children jostle in a queue | ● Determine the routes bathers take from the point of entry to the pool hall to any water features and whether these will take bathers near to deep water<br><br>● Determine whether water slide users have to queue close to deep water<br><br>● Determine the route water slide users take from the slide splashdown pool, or catch unit, and whether this will take them close to deep water | 1 Reconsider circulation routes<br><br>2 Control circulation routes using physical barriers to force bathers to use appropriate route<br><br>3 Provide physical barriers where queues are likely to form near deep water<br><br>4 If space is available, provide barrier rails to separate the main pool and water slide circulation<br><br>5 Close off short cuts that take bathers near deep water<br><br>6 Train staff to be vigilant of this issue |

| Identify design problem and hazards which may arise | Examine design problem - examples of checks which can be made | Examples of options for control |
|---|---|---|
| | | 7 Reconsider water feature usage patterns to reduce queuing |
| **1.3 Narrow pool surrounds (ie less than 2 m) cause congestion and restrict access. For small pools, this may be less than 1.5 m**<br><br>Inadequate width may cause crowding during busy periods and, if further restricted by handrails on steps or ladders, may prevent easy access along the pool surround for wheelchair users | ● Establish which surrounds are less than the recommended minimum width and whether this causes any serious problems with congestion or prevents easy access<br><br>● Establish whether there is sufficient circulation space between the handrails and walls<br><br>● Check whether the handrails are of the removable type<br><br>● Consult handrail manufacturer/supplier for most appropriate type | 1 Replace handrails with a design that does not protrude into the surround or with a removable type<br><br>2 If the problem is serious, consider management methods to control congestion |
| **1.4 Abrupt changes in floor level, eg steps, footbaths, upstands (to contain shower or hosing-down water)**<br><br>May cause bathers to trip or slip and lose their balance | ● Check whether the hazard is clearly visible to bathers with impaired vision<br><br>● Check whether any finishes that form part of the hazard are slippery<br><br>● Check whether any step treads are slippery and, if so, determine why, for example, the surface is worn, the surface has little or no slip-resistance, or the method of cleaning is inadequate or inappropriate<br><br>● Check whether bathers are able to easily negotiate the hazard and whether handrails would be helpful<br><br>● Check whether the hazard can be physically removed; obtain professional advice on the structural implications of doing this | 1 Provide high-visibility marking or tiling at all changes in floor level<br><br>2 Ensure the nosings to any steps are slip-resistant and are colour-contrasted for improving their visibility<br><br>3 Ensure any step treads have a slip-resistant surface<br><br>4 Provide handrails to both sides of any steps<br><br>5 Provide good illumination that allows the change in level to be clearly identified<br><br>6 Provide warning signs at the change in level and at appropriate points in the pool building<br><br>7 Provide alternative means to footbath for cleaning. Fill in footbath with new floor construction/finish to match existing finish |

| Identify design problem and hazards which may arise | Examine design problem - examples of checks which can be made | Examples of options for control |
|---|---|---|
| | | 8 If practicable, remove all upstands to shower areas and make good the areas from which the upstands were removed. Ensure that the floor finishes on either side of the upstands are level with each other and that the new infill floor finish matches the existing finish |
| **1.5 Ramped access between changes in floor level, eg pool surrounds adjacent to wave machine chamber**<br><br>May cause bathers to slip and lose their balance. If the ramp is located adjacent to the pool tank, this could cause a bather to fall from a high freeboard into the pool, risking serious injury | ● Establish whether the ramp gradient exceeds the maximum recommended gradient of 1 in 15<br><br>● Establish whether the ramp finish is sufficiently slip-resistant and is suitable for the ramp gradient (see also item 5 'Floors' for recommended options)<br><br>● Check whether the top and bottom of the ramp are clearly visible to bathers with impaired vision<br><br>● Check whether the side of the ramp is open to the pool and whether bathers can slip into the water | 1 Provide high-visibility floor marking at the top and bottom of the ramp<br><br>2 Provide handrails to both sides of the ramp. Where ramps are positioned adjacent to the pool tank, the handrail can be designed with additional rails or infill panels, to prevent bathers from jumping or falling off the ramp<br><br>3 Provide an alternative, temporary floor covering (eg ribbed plastic matting) to the ramp. Consult floor covering manufacturer/ supplier on suitability, water drainage, slip resistance and cleaning needs<br><br>4 Provide warning signs. |
| **1.6 Freestanding columns/ features block views**<br><br>Sight lines may be obstructed, making effective supervision difficult | ● Check whether lifeguarding positions have clear view of all areas | 1 If necessary, reposition staff or provide additional staff so that they have clear views<br><br>2 Remove or modify feature; obtain professional advice on the implications of doing this |

| Identify design problem and hazards which may arise | Examine design problem - examples of checks which can be made | Examples of options for control |
|---|---|---|
| **1.7 Projecting/freestanding columns or features such as pool covers interfere with circulation and/or present an impact hazard** | • Check whether the circulation space is adequate for two bathers to pass each other comfortably, ie 1.5 m | 1 If practicable, consider removing unnecessary obstructions to achieve clear space. If the building structure is affected, obtain professional advice on the most appropriate solution |
| Projecting/freestanding elements which seriously reduce the acceptable circulation space can be a hazard

Projecting or freestanding columns with sharp edges or corners may cause injury | • Check whether the corners and edges of any elements are sharp and are in a position that could injure a passing bather | 2 Provide high-visibility marking and impact-absorbing finish (eg padding) to unmovable/fixed elements. Ensure any corners are chamfered or rounded

3 Provide a wall-mounted pool cover (ie approximately 2.5 m above the pool surround level). Obtain professional advice on whether the supporting structure is strong enough to support the additional loading |
| **1.8 Inadequate spacing between rows of lockers and/or lockers and cubicles**

Locker doors in an open position might cause injury | • Check whether the aisle width meets the recommended minimum space of 1.5 m ie between parallel rows of lockers. This can be reduced to 1.2 m between parallel rows of cubicles and lockers, although 1.5 m is preferred

• Check whether the locker doors in their open position are likely to be a hazard to children | 1 If space is available, reposition lockers/cubicles to meet these dimensions

2 Consult locker manufacturer/supplier on the most appropriate method of keeping doors in closed position, for example by the use of falling hinges

3 Replace lockers with echelon design arrangement

4 Provide warning signs |

| Identify design problem and hazards which may arise | Examine design problem - examples of checks which can be made | Examples of options for control |
|---|---|---|
| **1.9 Areas of the pool hall which are access is difficult, eg high freeboards, 'islands' in leisure waters, or pool surround areas that are cut off by physical barriers such as water-slides, planting or guard-rails**<br><br>May cause delay in treating an injured person | ● Establish location of areas difficult to access<br><br>● Determine those parts of the pool surround that are suitable for landing a casualty, including the best route(s) for transporting the casualty from the pool surround to the first-aid room and ambulance parking | 1  Prepare/obtain from pool designer a layout of the overall pool hall indicating these areas and also those parts of the pool surround that are suitable for landing a casualty, including the best route to the first-aid facility and ambulance parking area<br><br>2  Make staff aware of the best routes for removing a casualty and brief ambulance/paramedic personnel, if required |
| **1.10 Inadequate and/or badly positioned first-aid facilities and access for emergency vehicles**<br><br>Injured people may have to be transferred to a place of treatment via an inconvenient/hazardous route | ● Establish whether there are any physical barriers or obstructions which prevent an injured person from being moved from the accident location to the first-aid room and, if there are, whether there is an alternative route(s)<br><br>● Establish the best route for carrying a stretcher from the first-aid room/pool surround to an external point accessible to emergency vehicles<br><br>● Examine possible ways of providing an external, designated hardstanding area for emergency vehicles that is close to the first-aid room | 1  Make staff aware of the best routes for removing a casualty and ensure they can brief ambulance/paramedic personnel, if required<br><br>2  If there are problems in achieving a reasonable solution, there may be a need to consider relocating the first-aid room, or providing additional first-aid facilities. Obtain professional advice on the most appropriate solution |

| Identify design problem and hazards which may arise | Examine design problem - examples of checks which can be made | Examples of options for control |
|---|---|---|

## 2 Walls

| | | |
|---|---|---|
| **2.1 Abrasive wall finishes adjacent to 'wet' circulation areas, ie from floor level to 2 m**<br><br>Cuts and other injuries | ● Evaluate accident record of pool to determine whether remedial action is required<br><br>● Check whether any masonry walls have abrasive surfaces and/or sharp edges and whether the joints are flush or recessed<br><br>● If necessary, consider options for providing a flush, smooth finish for a height of 2 m from floor level | 1 Masonry walls should have flush or bucket-handled joints for a height of 2 m from finished floor level. Obtain professional advice on the practicability of providing a flush surface<br><br>2 If space is available, construct a new flush wall with its finished surface positioned in front of the abrasive finish. Obtain professional advice on the design and best form of construction<br><br>3 Provide guard-rails to prevent bathers from coming into contact with the abrasive finish |
| **2.2 Sharp corners/edges to projections and/or openings**<br><br>Cuts and other injuries | ● Evaluate accident record of pool to determine whether remedial action is required<br><br>● Check whether there are any sharp corners/edges to any projecting wall elements and/or wall openings | 1 Replace corner elements with round-edged finishes/elements eg tiles, bull-nosed bricks<br><br>2 Cover corners with new, smooth, round-edged lining material. Obtain professional advice on the best options for achieving this<br><br>3 If space is available, construct a new flush wall with its finished surface positioned in front of any projecting structural columns by filling the recesses between the columns. Obtain professional advice on the design and best form of construction<br><br>4 Cover any projections or abrasive wall finishes with a new flush surface material for a height of 2 m from finished floor level. Ensure any corners are chamfered or rounded |

| Identify design problem and hazards which may arise | Examine design problem - examples of checks which can be made | Examples of options for control |
|---|---|---|
| **2.3 Projecting equipment such as fire extinguishers, fire hose reels**<br><br>Might cause injury | • Evaluate accident record of pool to determine whether remedial action is required<br><br>• Check whether they protrude into the circulation space | 1 Reposition so that equipment is not protruding into the circulation space<br><br>2 Reposition in wall recess/accessible duct |
| **2.4 Power sockets positioned at low level**<br><br>Electric shock, possibly leading to death | • Determine whether the electrical installation meets the latest edition of BS 7671[12] (also known as the IEE Regulations). The type of socket specified must be resistant to moisture. The circuit and sockets must be protected with a residual current circuit-breaker<br><br>• Evaluate need for sockets in wet areas | 1 Reposition sockets so that they are not accessible and/or are tamperproof<br><br>2 Replace sockets which do not comply with the IEE Regulations |
| **2.5 Low-level radiators/ heating pipes**<br><br>Body burns, particularly to young children | • Check positions of any radiators, particularly where they are located in tight areas<br><br>• Check type of radiator/ heater. | 1 Replace with low surface-temperature radiators or convector-type heaters<br><br>2 Reroute pipes so that they are not accessible to young children<br><br>3 Obtain professional advice on the most appropriate type and the best solution for repositioning any pipework |

## 3 Glazing

| | | |
|---|---|---|
| **3.1 Glazing in the pool hall which does not comply with specified standard**<br><br>Danger of severe injury or death from non-safety glazing being used, caused by impact from inside or outside the pool | • Determine type of glazing used for any glazed areas, including doors, windows and glazed screens. | 1 Replace non-compliant glazing with suitably toughened safety glazing to relevant standards. Obtain professional advice on the most suitable solution<br><br>2 Provide barrier rail(s) to prevent bathers from coming into contact with the glazing<br><br>3 If the pool is used for water polo, provide protective netting to prevent ball impact |

| Identify design problem and hazards which may arise | Examine design problem - examples of checks which can be made | Examples of options for control |
|---|---|---|
| **3.2 Window design/ positioning causes excessive glare and specular reflection**<br><br>Staff cannot easily see bathers on the surface or under the water | • Determine extent of problem to poolside staff by observing how the source of glare affects visibility of the pool tank bottom when viewed from the pool surrounds. This check should be carried out at different times of the day and year when the sun is in different positions to assess the extent of the problem | 1  Reposition poolside staff so that they are facing away from the source of glare. Consider need to improve ventilation, if staff are likely to be affected by solar gain<br><br>2  Provide blinds to control amount of light<br><br>3  Reduce the extent of the glazing. Obtain professional advice on possible options for achieving this<br><br>4  Replace clear glazing with heavily tinted glass. Consult building designer for the most suitable glass<br><br>5  Provide external planting to filter light |

## 4 Signs

| | | |
|---|---|---|
| **4.1 Poor placement of water depth signs**<br><br>Bathers may enter or progress into water of an unsafe depth (for them) if they cannot see or read depth markings | • Establish whether the existing signs meet the recommended requirements and are clearly visible to bathers, both on the pool surrounds and in the water. Refer to Appendix 2 for details<br><br>• Check whether all water areas have water depth signs<br><br>• Check whether the signs can be read by bathers with visual impairment<br><br>• Check whether the signs include pictorial elements for non-readers | 1  If necessary, provide clear signage at all appropriate points depending on pool configuration, including point of entry into pool<br><br>2  'No diving' signs should be placed so as to clearly indicate where diving is prohibited because of the water depth<br><br>3  Where it is impractical to provide wall-mounted signs that are clearly legible to bathers on the pool surrounds (for example, because the pool hall perimeter walls/ supporting structure are distant from the pool tank or various water areas are linked closely together, but are of different water depths), consider the provision of floor signs located on the pool surround itself, and, pictorial information positioned within the changing rooms and/or close to the point of entry to the pool hall |

| Identify design problem and hazards which may arise | Examine design problem - examples of checks which can be made | Examples of options for control |
|---|---|---|
| | | 4 Consider the provision of suspended overhead depth banners. Their design and positioning must ensure that they are clearly visible to bathers both in the water and on the surrounds, and that they are not confused with decorative banners |

**Floors**

| | | |
|---|---|---|
| **5.1 Slippery floor finish**<br><br>May cause bathers to slip and fall | • Evaluate accident record to assess the seriousness of the problem<br><br>• Establish whether the slip resistance of the floor finish is appropriate for wet bare feet and shod feet in both wet and dry conditions at the present floor gradient. Advice from the floor finish manufacturer and an independent testing laboratory may be required to establish this and recommend remedial action<br><br>• If a ceramic floor finish is installed, determine from the floor-finish manufacturer whether the finish was graded in terms of its slip resistance according to German Standard DIN 51097 (ie group A, B or C-A being the least resistant and C the most resistant). If the grading can be established, this will give an indication of whether the finish is appropriate for its location<br><br>• Establish whether the gradient of the floor effectively drains away any surface water. The maximum gradient of 1 in 35 for floors and 1 in 15 for ramps should not be exceeded. If there is a problem, obtain advice from the floor-finish manufacturer, and the pool | 1 Consult the project designer and floor-surface manufacturer/supplier for the most suitable solution<br><br>2 As a temporary solution, provide ribbed plastic matting of the rigid type and/or warning signs |

| Identify design problem and hazards which may arise | Examine design problem - examples of checks which can be made | Examples of options for control |
|---|---|---|
| | designer, on whether the slip resistance of the surface is satisfactory at the present gradient | |
| | ● Check whether there are any indentations in the surface where water can collect (ie surface ponding) | |
| | ● Establish whether the surfaces of any floor gullies/channels provide the same degree of slip resistance as the adjoining floor finish and whether there have been any accidents at these positions. If there have, consult the project designer and floor-surface manufacturer for the most suitable solution | |
| | ● Check whether the finish has been properly cleaned, thoroughly degreased and its surface is not worn. If it is badly worn, or has been repaired in various areas, the entire finish may need to be replaced by one with the appropriate degree of slip resistance. Obtain advice from the floor-finish manufacturer on appropriate cleaning methods | |
| | ● Check whether different floor finishes have been used in the same area. If so, there may be a need to replace one or both finishes with one finish | |
| **5.2 Sharp or raised edges, eg uneven tiling, drainage gullies/channels**<br><br>Sharp edges to finishes adjacent to movement joints may cut feet<br><br>Drainage gullies with projecting covers/gratings may cut feet | ● Evaluate accident record of pool to determine whether remedial action is required<br><br>● Establish whether the top of all movement joints are flush with adjacent floor finishes and whether any of the joint filler is missing<br><br>● Ensure any exposed edges to drainage gullies/ channels (ie metal or tile) are not sharp and they are set flush with adjoining floor surfaces | 1 As a temporary measure, cordon off affected floor area(s) to prevent bathers walking over them<br><br>2 Consult building designer and movement-joint manufacturer/supplier for cause of problem and to determine the most suitable solution |

| Identify design problem and hazards which may arise | Examine design problem - examples of checks which can be made | Examples of options for control |
|---|---|---|

## 6 Pool tanks generally

| Identify design problem and hazards which may arise | Examine design problem - examples of checks which can be made | Examples of options for control |
|---|---|---|
| **6.1 Slippery tank floor finish, particularly in shallow water areas eg the beach of a leisure pool**<br><br>May cause bathers to slip and fall | ● Establish whether the slip resistance of the finish and its gradient are appropriate for the location (for example by evaluating the accident record) | 1  Consult pool designer. Advice from the flooring manufacturer and an independent testing laboratory may be required to establish this and recommend remedial action<br><br>2  As a temporary measure provide warning signs |
| **6.2 Excessive pool tank gradient, ie greater than 1 in 15**<br><br>An excessive gradient may increase the likelihood of slipping and cause young children to be 'led' into deep water | ● Check whether the pool gradient exceeds the maximum recommended gradient of 1 in 15 and whether this occurs in a water depth of less than 1.5 m. If it does, consider measures listed | 1  Ensure that areas of steep gradient are clearly marked using coloured pool tank floor markings<br><br>2  Provide warning signs |
| **6.3 Abrupt changes in water depth where the water depth is less than 1.5 m eg steps beneath the water or steep changes in water depth between two water areas that are located close together**<br><br>May cause bathers to slip or to move into deep water | ● Check whether all changes in floor level can be clearly identified | 1  Ensure all step treads can be clearly identified by colour-contrasting the top edge (ie the nosing) of each step<br><br>2  Provide warning signs of any sudden changes in water depth<br><br>3  Consider possibility of introducing a physical barrier or water feature between the changes in water depth. Obtain professional advice to establish whether or not this is feasible and to advise on its design and construction |
| **6.4 Grille openings may lead to entrapment of fingers**<br><br>May lead to injury and drowning | ● Check size of apertures; for existing pools, they should not exceed 8 mm | 1  Consider replacing with grilles that have the appropriate aperture<br><br>2  Obtain advice from a building services engineer and/or a water treatment specialist on feasibility of replacing the existing grilles |

| Identify design problem and hazards which may arise | Examine design problem - examples of checks which can be made | Examples of options for control |
|---|---|---|
| **6.5 Excessive suction at outlets may cause entrapment** | ● Check the level of suction. Suction may trap parts of the body, which may lead to injury and drowning at each outlet. The number and positioning of outlets, net free surface area of the outlet covers and velocity of pumped outlet water should meet the requirements set out in the *Swimming pool water-treatment and quality standards*[13] <br><br> ● Obtain advice from a building services engineer and/or a water treatment specialist on the most appropriate solution for dealing with the problem | 1 Carry out measures recommended by building services engineer/water treatment specialist |
| **6.6 Sharp exposed edges to tiled finish, including cracked/broken and/or missing tiles, particularly at tile expansion joint positions** <br><br> Removal of expansion joint filler or grout erosion in tiled pools may expose sharp edges of tiles, causing body cuts | ● Evaluate accident record of pool to determine whether remedial action is required <br><br> ● Establish cause of problem, eg the tile expansion joints have not been constructed properly or do not coincide with the structural movement joints; damage to tiles may have been caused by canoe paddles <br><br> ● Establish cause of grout erosion, eg chemical and/or mechanical. Obtain advice from tile manufacturer and, if necessary, from an independent testing laboratory | 1 If feasible, consult building designer/structural engineer together with tile and sealant manufacturer for the most appropriate solution <br><br> 2 Replace with suitable grout only when cause of grout loss has been established <br><br> 3 Replace all cracked/broken tiles only when cause of problem has been resolved |
| **6.7 Poor definition of pool edge** <br><br> May cause injury to swimmers colliding with it in the water or when jumping into the tank from the pool surround | ● Check whether the pool edge is colour-contrasted with the colour of the pool tank and if necessary, the pool surround. If the colour of the pool surround finish contrasts with the colour of the pool tank finish, there should not be a problem | 1 Obtain advice from the pool designer and surround tile manufacturer on the most appropriate method of providing a better definition <br><br> 2 If a deck-level overflow channel is installed close to the pool edge, consider changing the grating for one with a colour that contrasts with the pool surrounds and tank |

| Identify design problem and hazards which may arise | Examine design problem - examples of checks which can be made | Examples of options for control |
|---|---|---|
| **6.8 Projecting rest ledges or handrails**<br><br>May present a hand or foot trap to bathers. In pools with a wave machine, the wave action may cause these features to be a hazard to bathers<br><br>Wave action in leisure pools may cause bathers to hit the handrail<br><br>Collisions by bathers jumping or falling into the pool | • Establish whether it is feasible to remove any projecting handrails, ie the pool edge will need to be within easy reach of bathers in the pool and provide a good hand hold<br><br>• Check whether the space between the handrail and the pool tank wall is large enough to withdraw an entrapped limb<br><br>• Establish whether the rest ledge is clearly visible from the pool surround | 1 If possible, remove any projecting handrails<br><br>2 Replace the ledge finish with colour-contrasted tiles<br><br>3 Provide warning signs of any projecting rest ledges |
| **6.9 Design of access ladder handrails and treads**<br><br>Excessive movement of hand-rails and/or narrow treads may cause bathers to lose their balance and/or get a limb trapped | • Determine whether there is excessive movement with the handrails and/or steps where these are integral with the handrails, and the cause of the movement, for example the ladder design is not sufficiently rigid and/or the handrails are not firmly fixed to the pool surround and tank wall<br><br>• Determine whether the treads are of sufficient slip resistance and width and whether they pose any problems for users, particularly elderly people<br><br>• Establish whether the space behind the back face of the step treads and the pool tank wall is likely to cause entrapment. Check the latest European Standard on swimming pool equipment in relation to the recommended dimensional requirements | 1 Consult building designer and/or the ladder manufacturer to determine the most sensible solution<br><br>2 Replace or modify ladders as recommended by the building designer/ladder manufacturer |
| **6.10 Projecting steps**<br><br>Lane swimmers may collide with projecting steps | • Check positioning of steps and whether they are likely to cause a problem | 1 Provide replacement steps which provide safe entry and exit with, if possible, reduced projection |

| Identify design problem and hazards which may arise | Examine design problem - examples of checks which can be made | Examples of options for control |
|---|---|---|
| **6.11 Concealed or difficult-to-observe water areas**<br><br>Bathers may get into difficulties out of sight of lifeguards | • Check whether all water areas can be supervised from the existing lifeguard positions | 1 Reposition staff, if necessary, so that all water areas can be easily supervised<br><br>2 Provide additional supervision to ensure that area is properly observed |
| **6.12 Fixed raised pool ends**<br><br>Misuse by untrained divers or bathers may lead to serious injury | • Check whether this feature is adequately supervised | 1 Ensure staff supervision covers these features<br><br>2 Where the water depth is less than 1.5 m, provide 'no diving' safety signs<br><br>3 Consider the provision of removable guard-rails. Consult building designer for most appropriate solution |
| **6.13 Permanent starting platforms**<br><br>Misuse by untrained divers may leading to serious injury<br><br>Tripping and collision hazard | • Check whether this feature is adequately supervised<br><br>• Consider alternative solutions for preventing unauthorised use of the platforms | 1 Remove from poolside and replace with demountable starting platforms. If this is not practicable, provide removable covers which prevent access to the platforms and their unauthorised use for diving<br><br>2 Provide 'no diving' safety signs |
| **6.14 Underwater features or fittings**<br><br>Projecting fittings or parts for water features might cause trips or might trap feet or hands<br><br>Projecting lane rope hooks may lead to injury | • Check whether there are any features in water depths up to 1.5 m that may cause a bather to trip<br><br>• Check whether there are any sharp projections that could lead to injury | 1 Remove projecting elements and replace, if feasible, with recessed alternatives<br><br>2 Ensure hooks are recessed behind the face of the pool tank wall/overflow channel. If this is not practicable, remove lane hooks |

| Identify design problem and hazards which may arise | Examine design problem - examples of checks which can be made | Examples of options for control |
|---|---|---|
| **6.15 'Wild water' or rapids features terminating near deep water and/or affecting water movement in other water areas**<br><br>Inexperienced bathers attracted to the feature being discharged into water beyond their depth | • Check water depth at point where bathers are discharged and whether this is likely to create difficulties for non-swimmers and/or young children<br><br>• Check whether the flow of water in the 'wild water' or rapids affects the flow of water in other water areas and causes non-swimmers and young children to be drawn into deep water | 1 Provide warning signage regarding level of bather ability at entry to water feature<br><br>2 Provide additional staff supervision at the exit point and if necessary, at the other water areas affected by water movement |
| **6.16 Misuse of a water feature**<br><br>Creates unsafe conditions in the pool either directly or by creating distraction and alarm | • Observe how the water feature is misused (or anticipate how it could be misused) and consider whether it is feasible to modify or remove that part of the feature causing the problem<br><br>• Consult feature manufacturer and/or the pool designer on the most appropriate solution | 1 Modify water feature to prevent misuse, or withdraw entirely |
| **6.17 High freeboard substantially greater than 380 mm, ie for example adjacent to wave machine chamber**<br><br>Bathers may want to rest against the side of the pool in areas of deep water<br><br>Bathers may jump/dive from this elevated position, increasing the potential risk of serious injury to themselves from impact with the pool bottom | • Check height of freeboard (ie the vertical distance between the water level and the pool surround) around the complete pool perimeter and note those parts of the surround that are higher than 380 mm. In leisure pools with wave machines, these are likely to be adjacent to the wave machine chamber, where the freeboard may exceed 1 m | 1 Provide a grab-rail at water level; ideally, this should be recessed flush with the pool tank walls, although this will not be practical with an existing pool<br><br>2 Provide a barrier rail along the length of the freeboard to prevent bathers from entering the pool tank<br><br>3 Take measures to prevent bathers from gaining access to those parts of the surround adjacent to the wave machine chamber, ie by barrier rails with gate access for staff<br><br>4 Provide signs prohibiting diving |

| Identify design problem and hazards which may arise | Examine design problem - examples of checks which can be made | Examples of options for control |
|---|---|---|

## 7 Diving pools

| Identify design problem and hazards which may arise | Examine design problem - examples of checks which can be made | Examples of options for control |
|---|---|---|
| **7.1 Pool tank and diving equipment which do not meet current ASA/FINA recommended standards**<br><br>A pool which is too shallow, poorly equipped, or with an unsafe layout of boards and platforms will put divers at risk of serious injury or death. If a movable floor has been installed, the water depth may not meet the recommended standards | ● Check pool and equipment dimensions, including their location. Information on the latest standards may be obtained from the ASA (see Appendix 7 for contact details) | 1 Take measures to prevent board(s) from being used<br><br>2 Restrict the nature of the activity permitted in the pool to that which it can safely accommodate<br><br>3 Remove diving platforms that are affected by reduced water depth and clearances |
| **7.2 Glare or other visual disturbance to divers**<br><br>Divers may be distracted at critical moments | ● Consult ASA and/or obtain professional advice regarding the examples of the measures referred to under options for control | 1 Provide screens which eliminate glare from light sources<br><br>2 Where possible, provide blinds to windows and/or glazed screens through which distracting movements can be seen<br><br>3 Consider temporary measures during competitive events and training |
| **7.3 Access to diving equipment**<br><br>Divers may lose their footing in wet conditions<br><br>Unauthorised access by an inexperienced bather may lead to serious injury<br><br>No method of restricting use | ● Check equipment, particularly the physical condition of any staircases, springboards and platforms. Establish whether the treads are sufficiently slip-resistant and the guard-rail and platform design will prevent divers from falling from the structure<br><br>● Check whether the floor surface finish, to the platforms, in particular, is worn and whether it needs to be replaced<br><br>● Consult ASA and/or obtain advice from the diving equipment supplier or designer | 1 Take measures to prevent access to diving equipment, eg fit gate(s) at foot of access stairs/ladders<br><br>2 Fit guard-rails to all access steps above 2 m in height<br><br>3 Ensure the finish to the treads to any access stairs, including the platforms, are sufficiently slip-resistant. Replace any worn finishes<br><br>4 Provide signs indicating who should use the boards<br><br>5 Brief staff on potential problems |

| Identify design problem and hazards which may arise | Examine design problem - examples of checks which can be made | Examples of options for control |
|---|---|---|
| **7.4 Swimming beneath diving boards**<br><br>Divers may collide with those who are leaving the pool having completed their dive | • Check overall equipment layout and establish the route divers take after completing their dive<br><br>• Check whether they use the access steps and whether these are positioned so that they have a safe exit route after completing their dive | 1 Ensure that access steps are placed so as to provide an exit route away from the diving area<br><br>2 Provide signs indicating how boards may be used<br><br>3 Brief staff on problem |
| **7.5 Diving pool is close to the shallow end of a main or learner pool**<br><br>Casual bathers, and particularly children, may fall into the deep water of the diving pool | • Check width of pool surround dividing the two water areas and extent of the deep water area. This may determine the position, extent and type of physical barrier to be provided | 1 If space is available, provide a physical barrier between the two water areas<br><br>2 Ensure effective control of access to the diving pool<br><br>3 Provide warning signs<br><br>4 Brief staff on problem |

## 8 Learner/training pools

| | | |
|---|---|---|
| **8.1 Unprotected access steps**<br><br>Possible injury caused by bathers jumping on to the steps from the pool surround | • Check whether it is possible for bathers to jump from the pool surrounds on to the pool access steps | 1 Provide guard-rails at the ends of the steps, ie where their ends adjoin the pool surrounds<br><br>2 Provide warning signs |
| **8.2 Narrow treads to the access steps and/or steep risers**<br><br>May cause slips and trips by children or those carrying children | • Check the width and height (ie the riser) of all access steps. The steps should be gently graded with risers of no greater than 140 mm and treads of 300 mm minimum<br><br>• Check whether there are sufficient handrails provided to help entry/exit. For wide flights of steps, the handrails should not be wider than 1.8 m apart | 1 Replace with wider and shallower steps with the minimum projection into the pool tank. Ideally, these should be recessed within the pool surround, although this will not be practicable with existing tanks except when they are being remodelled<br><br>2 Ensure the edges of all the step treads are colour-contrasted with the pool surround and tank and the treads are slip-resistant<br><br>3 Ensure there are sufficient handrails |

| Identify design problem and hazards which may arise | Examine design problem - examples of checks which can be made | Examples of options for control |
|---|---|---|

## 9 Water slides

| | | |
|---|---|---|
| **9.1 Clear headroom reduced at positions where bathers can pass underneath the slide and/or its supporting structure**<br><br>Bathers may collide with the slide and/or its supporting structure, causing head injuries | • Establish whether there is sufficient headroom for bathers; ideally, there should be 2 m clear between the floor and the lowest point of the slide and/or its supporting structure | 1 Provide impact-absorbing padding with high-visibility marking to any part of the slide and/or its structure, which is below this level.<br><br>2 Provide warning signs |
| **9.2 Slide splashdown pool does not meet latest standards**<br><br>Undersized pools might be a potential cause of accidents | • Check the overall dimensions of the tank, including the falling distance and water depth, and establish whether these meet the latest European Standard | 1 Evaluate the accident record of the pool to determine whether remedial action is required<br><br>2 If necessary, consider an alternative solution such as a catch unit. Consult pool designer and slide manufacturer on the design/structural implications of physically changing the pool and existing slide |
| **9.3 Slide terminates in pool with other uses**<br><br>Impacts caused by slide users clashing with other bathers | • Establish whether the dimensions of the splashdown area are similar to the dimensions required for a dedicated splashdown pool (as determined by the latest European Standard); also that the splashdown area is physically separated from the surrounding water area | 1 Provide clear demarcation between pool areas, allowing sufficient safe clearance for the splashdown area<br><br>2 Provide additional supervision to ensure security of demarcation |
| **9.4 Access stairs are too narrow or too wide for safe queuing**<br><br>May lead to slips and falls. Wide stairs can cause problems if bathers try to pass each other | • Check the design of the stair and platform in relation to the requirements set by the latest European Standard. The dimensions of the stairs/ladders should also be considered in relation to the requirements set by the latest Building Regulations. Consult the pool designer and the slide manufacturer on the most appropriate solution for dealing with the problem | 1 If necessary, take remedial action, ie modify or replace the existing stair/ladder<br><br>2 If too wide, provide barrier rails to separate circulation |

| Identify design problem and hazards which may arise | Examine design problem - examples of checks which can be made | Examples of options for control |
|---|---|---|
| **9.5 Slide platform is too small or is not adequately guarded**<br><br>Staff should be able to stand on the platform to control slide entry. Absence of appropriate guard-rails may lead to slips and falls | ● Check whether the design of the platform and the start section of the slide meet the recommendations given in the latest European Standard<br><br>● Consult the pool designer and the slide manufacturer on the most appropriate solution for dealing with the problem | 1 Provide guard-rails to prevent falls and to channel slide users correctly<br><br>2 Consider alternative management arrangements if member of staff cannot use platform<br><br>3 Consider replacement of platform |
| **9.6 Exit steps in splashdown pool are badly positioned**<br><br>Impacts between slide users caused by bathers being discharged from the end of the slide clashing with those leaving the splashdown pool | ● Check whether the position of the exit steps meets the recommendations given in the latest European Standard<br><br>● Consult the pool designer and the slide manufacturer on the most appropriate solution for dealing with the problem | 1 Relocate steps to the side of the splashdown pool opposite to that where the slide discharges the rider, ie to encourage riders to leave the pool away from the landing area.<br><br>2 Instigate management system which ensures that last bather has left the pool before next ride begins |
| **9.7 Poor sight lines from launch platform to splashdown area**<br><br>Slide users may collide in the splashdown area or on the slide if they are released before the previous user has exited, with risk of serious injury | ● Check whether the splashdown area is clearly visible from the launch platform | 1 If necessary, install one or more of these systems<br><br>2 Ensure staff fully understand how these systems operate<br><br>3 Consider alternative systems of management control such as, for example, traffic lights activated by the previous rider or staff positioned at the slide splashdown area (traffic lights operated by a timer are not acceptable), CCTV to enable staff to see users exit before releasing the next rider, or direct two-way communication between staff located at the launch platform and splashdown area<br><br>4 Obtain independent professional advice on the most appropriate system |

| Identify design problem and hazards which may arise | Examine design problem - examples of checks which can be made | Examples of options for control |
|---|---|---|
| **9.8 Water circulation inlets/ outlets are located where bathers land in splashdown area**<br><br>May cause injury, particularly if there are any projections or sharp edges | ● Check that any inlet/outlet grilles that are located in the landing area of riders are flush with the pool tank bottom and do not have any sharp edges<br><br>● Consult a building services engineer and/or filtration pipework/grill manufacturer on alternative solutions | 1 If necessary, replace the grilles with a flush-fitting type, ie one that does not protrude beyond the tank finish<br><br>2 Modify the existing outlets with the addition of a contoured attachment to produce a smooth profile |
| **9.9 Traps between water slide parts and fixed surrounding elements such as walls**<br><br>May trap slide or pool users, leading to injury or death | ● Check the clearance zones in relation to the requirements set by the latest European Standard<br><br>● Examine all intersections and junctions for traps. Consult pool designer and the slide manufacturer/ supplier on the most appropriate way of dealing with the problem | 1 If required, modify the slide design as recommended by the pool designer and slide manufacturer |

# Supervision arrangements to safeguard pool users

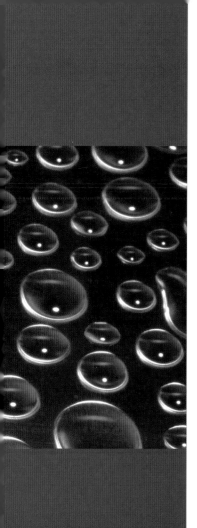

## Introduction

All pools require some measure of supervision but arrangements for each location must be determined by the risk assessment. The risk assessment undertaken at a swimming pool will need to include not only the physical hazards but those hazards relating to swimmers and swimming-related activities. When pool operators assess the need for supervision they will need to consider:

- local circumstances;
- the pool structure and equipment;
- the way the pool is used and the characteristics of those who may use it.

## Awareness of risks

In order to plan for safe procedures, pool operators will need to have an appreciation of the main hazards and risks to users. The following hazards/risks have been factors in past deaths or serious injuries:

- inadequate or inappropriate supervision;
- prior health problems (eg heart trouble, impaired hearing or sight, epilepsy);
- alcohol or food before swimming;
- youth and inexperience (half of those who drown are under the age of 15);

- weak or non-swimmers straying out of their depth;
- unauthorised access to pools intended to be out of use;
- diving into insufficient depth of water (leading to concussion, or injury to head or spine);
- unruly behaviour and misuse of equipment;
- unclear pool water, preventing casualties from being seen;
- absence of, or inadequate response by, lifeguards in an emergency.

**133** Careful recording and consideration of any incidents experienced at the pool will help to ensure that safety arrangements remain relevant. The NOP will need to draw attention to any particular risk factors. Certain kinds of incident must be reported to the appropriate enforcing authorities for health and safety legislation, see paragraphs 54 to 57.

**134** Pool operators may need to vary the arrangements for supervision from time to time, according to current use, eg public or teaching/coaching sessions, and this will be reflected in the NOP. Pool operators have a duty of care to the users of their premises. The duty of care applies to both staff and visitors and may need to vary according to specific contracts or the age of visitors. The duty of care will need to be greater in respect of children, and especially children with disabilities.

**135** Safe operation of pools generally requires the deployment of lifeguards. It is the responsibility of the pool operator to ensure that they are sufficient in number, adequately trained, effectively organised and diligent in their duties. This responsibility includes assessing whether hirers of pools have made effective and safe arrangements for supervision (see paragraphs 183-184 for further details).

**Prevention**

**136** Arguably, prevention is the most important duty of the pool lifeguard and can be achieved through encouraging pool users to act responsibly and in a safe manner.

*Prevention through education*

**137** Any pool will be safer if bathers are aware of potential hazards, and act responsibly. As far as is reasonably practicable, the hazards should be brought to bathers' attention as soon as possible. This can be achieved in a variety of ways, such as:

- notices displayed at reception, in changing areas and on the poolside;
- a leaflet handed to bathers as they arrive, and to those in charge of organised groups (including school parties);
- references in contracts with club organisers, schools, etc, hiring the pool;
- oral reminders, where necessary, by lifeguards.

**138** Lifeguards are in the front line of pool-user education and can help prevent accidents; therefore good communication skills are essential. Lifeguards can educate pool users about the hazards and risks associated with a particular pool or activity, and about water safety generally. An effective method is to firmly draw attention to clearly designed and well-placed signs.

*Prevention through supervision*

**139**  Constant poolside supervision by lifeguards provides the best assurance of pool-users' safety. Lifeguard training should include knowledge of pool supervision and supervision skills, and practical skills in scanning and observation. Effective supervision requires high levels of concentration and attentiveness and the length of duty spells on the poolside is one important factor affecting lifeguards.

**The pool lifeguard**

**140**  The term 'lifeguard' should only be applied to someone who possesses the attributes and competence necessary to fulfil the duties which are set out in this guidance. Pool operators should be aware that some hirers, volunteers or potential employees may consider themselves to be qualified to act as 'lifeguards' even though they do not have or understand the attributes and competence for such a role. This could lead to confusion and the appointment of unsuitable people. It is essential that the pool lifeguards understand their role, and are given adequate training (identified through the PSOP and arrived at through the risk assessment) to perform all the duties expected of them.

**141**  A lifeguard can be:

- an employee of the pool operator;
- carrying out lifeguard duties under a formal arrangement made by the hirer of the pool; or
- a volunteer.

The same requirements apply to anybody who acts as a lifeguard, whether or not they are paid to do so.

*Responsibilities of pool operators towards lifeguards*

**142**  Pool operators should ensure that lifeguards:

- are properly supervised;
- are clear about their duties and areas of work;
- know who is in charge at any time (this will be specified in the NOP);
- are provided with adequate training (to ensure competence is maintained) with assessment to a sufficient level at their centre which conforms to the Management of Health and Safety at Work Regulations 1992.

**Duties of a lifeguard**

**143**  The key functions of the lifeguard are to:

- keep a close watch over the pool and the pool users, exercising the appropriate level of control;
- communicate effectively with pool users, and colleagues;
- anticipate problems and prevent accidents;
- intervene to prevent behaviour which is unsafe;
- identify emergencies quickly and take appropriate action;
- effect a rescue from the water;

- give immediate first aid to any casualty;
- be able to supervise; paragraphs 148-180 provide further guidance in this area.

### *Resuscitation of casualties*

**144**  An essential skill required by a lifeguard attempting to carry out resuscitation is the ability to perform basic life support using the techniques of rescue breathing and chest compressions, together known as cardiopulmonary resuscitation (CPR).

### *Extended life support*

**145**  Pool operators should be aware, and apply as appropriate, approved methods of extended life support including the skills of oxygen insufflation and automated external defibrillation (AED).

### *Ensuring the safe management of spinal injuries*

**146**  A small, but nonetheless significant, number of accidents occur in swimming pools in which the casualty sustains a spinal injury.  When such an injury is suspected, it is essential that the methods used in rescuing the casualty from the pool and carrying out any subsequent attempt at resuscitation avoid making it worse. Accordingly, lifeguards should receive adequate training in awareness of spinal injuries so that they can ensure an absolute minimum of movement of the casualty's spine when they are moved and when ensuring a clear airway.

**147**  Specially designed spinal boards are available which support the whole of the casualty's body and prevent flexion of the spine when the casualty is removed from the water.  It is essential that where spinal boards are provided, lifeguards are trained, individually and as a team,  in their use, and practise their techniques on a regular basis.

### Requirements of a lifeguard

**148**  In order to perform the duties set out in paragraphs 143-147, lifeguards will need to:

- be physically fit, have good vision and hearing, be mentally alert and self-disciplined;
- be strong, able and confident swimmers;
- be trained and  have successfully completed a course of training in the techniques and practices of supervision, rescue and first aid in accordance with a syllabus approved by a recognised training organisation;
- receive a programme of induction (to include health and safety management) prior to undertaking their duties, and as specified by the pool operator;
- receive a programme of regular ongoing training.

### Physical fitness

**149**  A lifeguard should have a good level of physical fitness.  A lifeguard's level of hearing and vision should be appropriate to the environment in which he or she is working.  Pool operators will need to take this into account when carrying out their risk assessment and ensure that the lifeguard's standard of hearing and vision is such that it does not interfere with the duties the lifeguard has to undertake.

**Swimming ability**

It is strongly recommended that all lifeguards are sufficiently fit and have the ability to swim on their front for 100 m without stopping, and to swim 100 m on their back without stopping; and to swim 50 m within 60 seconds and to surface dive to a depth of a least 1.5 m. The risk assessment will determine what levels are needed for each pool where the requirements may be greater than stated here.

**Lifeguard training and qualifications**

*Training*

Under the MHSWR 1992, pool operators will need to assess the capabilities of their staff and ensure they are adequately trained for the duties they carry out. It is good practice to maintain written records for all training sessions which include: names of those involved; what they did, including use of equipment; and length of training sessions. Such records can be kept manually or held on computer.

All lifeguards need to be effectively trained to enable them to carry out their role and tasks efficiently and for the health, safety and welfare of all in their charge. Their duties should be suitably restricted and supervised until the necessary competence has been acquired.

There are a number of ways to ensure that employees receive adequate training and instruction such as on-the-job training and attendance at courses. Effective training will mean a firm base of knowledge and skills application which might reasonably be attributed to the needs of swimming pools in general, and in addition site-specific training which seeks to develop in the lifeguard a full understanding of the PSOP and facilities of a particular pool and how they should be used.

It is strongly recommended that pool lifeguards hold a current qualification issued by an appropriate national body (see Appendix 7) as it is a widely recognised way of demonstrating an acceptable level of competence. The standards achieved by pool lifeguards must at least reach the minimum level defined for the safe operation of swimming facilities.

*Pool lifeguard qualifications*

A pool lifeguard qualification requires two elements: core or foundation knowledge and skills as well as site-specific knowledge and skills. All lifeguards need frequent, suitable training, which should be recorded, to ensure the retention of these skills.

*Foundation or core training*

Procedures for qualifications should include:

- training by a qualified and competent person;
- independent assessment by a qualified and competent person;
- a test of knowledge and practical skills;
- an independent reassessment by a qualified and competent person at least every 24 months.

**157** Foundation or core training includes gaining both knowledge and practical skills in:

- fitness training with preparatory standard of swimming ability before starting a course (see paragraph 150);
- principles of PSOP;
- understanding pool features and pool activities;
- water safety and accident prevention;
- role of the lifeguard and responsibilities under the law;
- pool observation and supervision skills;
- drowning, dry drowning (in which no water reaches the lungs), secondary drowning (fluid in the lungs caused by irritation by inhaled water);
- use of poolside rescue equipment;
- communication methods and working as a team;
- casualty recognition, principles of rescue and manual handling;
- CPR, first aid and spinal cord injury management.

**158** The experience of the industry shows that in order to possess the necessary knowledge, skills and competence a significant number of recording training hours are required.

### Site specific training

**159** In addition to core skills, lifeguards must have knowledge and skills to be competent in the health and safety aspects of the specific location in which they work. These should relate to:

- the enactment of legislation, eg COSHH, HSW Act, RIDDOR, PPE;
- the swimming pool, its design features, equipment and storage, emergency equipment, cleanliness and hygiene, pool cleaning, pre-swim hygiene, pool water clarity, glare and blind spots, personal safety equipment;
- details of the PSOP, ie NOP and EAP;
- supervision skills;
- provision and use of play equipment;
- flumes, water slides and other water features;
- diving in pools.

**160** The site-specific elements of lifeguard competence and training take two forms: initial and ongoing.

### Initial training

**161** Initial training will help new lifeguards to become competent. It will include formal off-the-job training, instruction to individuals and groups and on-the-job coaching and counselling. Ensuring that people are competent may demand more than training, for example a period of supervised experience to practise and develop new skills. Formal evaluation by a qualified, competent person should be undertaken after each aspect of training to establish if the training objectives have been achieved. A record of the training and assessment process for each person should be maintained.

### In-service and ongoing staff training

**162**  To maintain the skills and competency of a lifeguard, suitable and sufficient training and competency assessment should be conducted regularly* by qualified training staff and will need to include:

- a fitness programme to include timed swims and towing and rescue methods;
- simulated incident training, working in a team, based on the site-specific EAP;
- a dive to the bottom of the deepest part of the pool to recover a simulated casualty (manikin);
- the use of poolside rescue equipment;
- revisions to the PSOP due to changed circumstances;
- refresher training in supervision and scanning techniques.

**163**  Records of the training undertaken and the objectives achieved for each individual should be maintained and be available for inspection by an authorised person.

**164**  Ongoing, regular, suitable and sufficient training and assessment should ensure the competency of lifeguards. This should be supplemented by a two-yearly, external test of core or foundation skills, given by a suitably competent person and provided as a means of assuring the authenticity and appropriateness of the ongoing training programme.

### Teachers and coaches of programmed sessions - safety qualification

**165**  A lifeguard may not be required in programmed sessions in a pool where the teaching and coaching of swimming is taking place. In these situations, where the risk is limited due to the nature of the activity and the degree of control exercised, the teacher or coach may provide the safety cover. However, they should have the appropriate teaching/coaching lifesaving competencies which include rescue skills, CPR, and relevant aspects of the PSOP.

**166**  Where teachers are directly responsible for supervising the swimming pool, performing the role of lifeguards in an unprogrammed pool session, they too should have the competencies and skills required of a lifeguard in those circumstances.

**167**  Appendix 7 lists the national bodies which provide safety training qualifications. These are the best way of showing competence, for teachers and coaches of swimming and related disciplines, when supervising programmed activities.

### Clothing

**168**  Lifeguards need to wear distinctive clothing so that they can easily be recognised in an emergency. They also need to carry whistles.

**169**  It is recommended that pool operators consider the clothing (uniform) worn by lifeguards when on duty. It needs to be distinctive and pool operators may wish to consider the internationally accepted colours of red shorts/skirt and yellow top. Clothing for lifeguards should be of a design appropriate to their role and should not hamper them during an in-water rescue.

---

* 'Regularly' means as required to suit the circumstances of the pool and sufficient to maintain competency. Medical authorities recommend that training in CPR takes place at least monthly.

When providing a uniform for staff at open-air pools, recognition must be given to the problems of prolonged exposure to the sun, and the cold and wet conditions which are often experienced. Where appropriate, a broad-brimmed hat, long-sleeved shirt and polarising sunglasses should be worn and sunblock preparations used.

**Deployment of lifeguards**

*Duty spells and structuring of duties*

 The length and structuring of duty spells require careful consideration by pool operators who should specify the maximum period of uninterrupted supervision, the length of the working day, and programmed breaks from duty. To maintain the high levels of vigilance and concentration required by lifeguards, pool operators should make allowance for any of the following factors when deciding the length of duty spells:

- features of pool design affecting vision, hearing or concentration;
- inappropriate illumination;
- problems of glare and reflection;
- inadequate ventilation system;
- poor acoustics;
- extreme temperatures or excessively high humidity, or hot sun in open pools, solar gain;
- water turbulence, crowded conditions and excessive noise will tend to increase risk;
- wave machines/flumes, features and other equipment;
- distractions from poolside activities, eg radios, ball games and similar activities.

 Any of these may suggest the need for an increase in the number of lifeguards and for a decrease in surveillance spells, for example when pools are close to capacity and where seasonal or other peak loading can be expected. This will need to be included in the NOP. Sometimes problems can be reduced by minor building improvements, eg localised ventilation, air flow at the start area to a water slide, sun shade on a high chair in open-air pools.

 There should be a formalised method, included in the NOP, for rotation between the poolside duties and duties away from the poolside and for rotation between lifeguarding duties at the poolside, which ensures that lifeguarding levels and supervision of all areas of the pool are maintained.

Where part-time or casual staff are employed or volunteers are used who may have other employment, or where full-time staff are known to have other employment, operators will need to satisfy themselves that the other employment does not interfere with the efficient performance of lifeguard duties, for example tiredness as a result of late-night employment which may affect vigilance.

*Lifeguard numbers*

 Given the wide range of pool facilities, and the ways pools are used, it is not possible to make specific recommendations for lifeguard numbers. Pool operators will need to consider what is required (this will be determined in the risk assessment) and take into account all relevant local circumstances at any particular time. The general arrangements decided upon will need to be set out in the NOP.

176 As a starting point for pool operators' consideration, Table 2 sets out suggested minimum numbers of lifeguards for certain standard sizes of rectangular pools, when used for unprogrammed swimming and without the use of diving boards or other special equipment. However, further consideration will need to be given to increasing the numbers of lifeguards on duty if special features are available or in operation. Fewer lifeguards may be required during lane/fitness swimming because of the higher competence level of swimmers.

**Table 2** Lifeguard numbers: basic guideline

| Approximate pool size: m | Area: m² | Minimum number of lifeguards | Recommended minimum number of lifeguards in busy conditions |
|---|---|---|---|
| 20.0 x 8.5 | 170 | 1 | 2 |
| 25.0 x 8.5 | 212 | 1 | 2 |
| 25.0 x 10.0 | 250 | 1 | 2 |
| 25.0 x 12.5 | 312 | 2 | 2 |
| 33.3 x 12.5 | 416 | 2 | 3 |
| 50.0 x 20.0 | 1000 | 4 | 6 |

**Notes to Table 2**

1    Where only one lifeguard is on duty at the poolside there should be adequate means, such as an alarm or some form of bleeper, of summoning assistance rapidly to the pool area. This is essential where a single lifeguard is involved in an in-water rescue. The remaining bathers are no longer supervised until backup lifeguards/staff arrive and the recovery of a casualty from the water often requires at least two people.

2    The figures in the fourth column are the recommended minimum whenever loading approaches pool maximum capacity (paragraphs 202-204).

3    For irregularly shaped pools, including many leisure pools, the figures in the second column of the table, related to the water area, may be a useful starting point.

4    In 50-metre pools where the width is 16 m or more, visibility through the water becomes a problem. In determining the number of lifeguards and their positioning, tests to check visibility should be made.

 177 Additional lifeguards may be required to cover all areas of water, including any which are physically separate, or 'hidden' by features.

 178 Fewer lifeguards may be required where a pool contains water of only 1 m or less in depth. Conversely, the presence of water deeper than 2 m, or unusually extensive areas of deep water, may require additional supervision.

*Surveillance/zones*

**179** All areas of the pool and its environs must be adequately observed and supervised. The pool should be divided into zones to ensure all areas are covered. Each zone will need to be continuously scanned. Zones will include the water area above and below the surface plus steps, ladders, activity equipment, walkways, entrances, and the poolside.

**180** Scanning is the skill required by lifeguards to constantly watch a particular zone using a sweeping action. They will need to be able to scan their zone of supervision in 10 seconds and to be close enough to get to an incident within 20 seconds. This is an internationally recognised practice and is known as the 10:20 system.

*Supervision of changing facilities*

**181** As with any part of the swimming pool an assessment of the health and safety risks to users within changing areas will also need to be undertaken. Hazards identified as being a risk will need to be eliminated or the risks reduced as far as possible. For example, pool operators will need to give consideration to what level of supervision or checking is required for:

- showers and other washing facilities;
- seating;
- floors;
- equipment (hairdryers, etc);
- toilets.

**182** Extra checks may be required if the changing area is particularly busy or there is a large number of unsupervised children, though this duty does not have to be undertaken by a fully qualified lifeguard.

**Responsibilities of the pool operator for lifeguard provision when the pool is hired to other people**

**183** When the pool is hired to outside organisations the same standards will apply and will need to be included in the PSOP (see Appendix 5).

**184** Where agreement is reached that the outside organisation will provide supervision, pool operators will need to consider what, if any, additional cover may be needed, bearing in mind that:

- they retain residual responsibilities for all those who use the pool and the facilities;
- where the hire organisation shares use of the pool with the general public, the pool operator retains sole responsibility for safety;
- it will usually be necessary for the pool operator to have a responsible person on the premises who is trained to discharge the operator's responsibilities;
- the standard of pool supervision should be detailed in the hiring agreement and the operator should ensure that the agreement is being met (through random checks, for example).

**Volunteers**

**185**
The pool operator remains responsible and must maintain control and will need to make appropriate enquiries about the volunteers' competence and level of training before allowing them to undertake voluntary work. Additional training which may be required will need to be agreed between the pool operator and the volunteer or organisation they represent in order to ensure that at all times the PSOP will be complied with. In essence, the competence of a volunteer will need to match that of the normal staff employed to undertake lifeguarding duties, including the relevant site-specific elements.

**Factors to consider when deciding whether constant poolside supervision is necessary**

**186**
Constant poolside supervision by lifeguards provides the best assurance of pool users' safety. The risk assessment may determine circumstances where the balance of cost and risk makes it possible to provide a safe swimming environment without constant poolside supervision. Before deciding this, pool operators should carefully consider relevant circumstances such as:

- the nature of the pool;
- the pool users;
- activities in the pool at any particular time.

**187**
A risk assessment must be undertaken to decide whether constant poolside supervision is required. If the pool meets one or more criteria from the following list, it is strongly recommended that constant poolside supervision is provided:

- the pool has water deeper than 1.5 m;
- the pool water area is greater than 170 m²;
- diving from the poolside is allowed;
- there is poolside equipment or a feature posing additional risk;
- there are abrupt changes in depth;
- it is not practicable to enforce house rules for safe behaviour;
- access is not restricted, eg as in hotel residents, members, hospital staff and patients.

**188**
Whether constant poolside supervision is required also depends on how a pool is used at any given time. For example, a pool which would not normally require poolside supervision may need to make arrangements for supervision on occasions when:

- the pool will be used by unaccompanied children aged under 15 years;
- crowded conditions are expected;
- food or alcohol will be available to pool users; or
- activities take place or equipment is used which can lead to additional risks through the high excitement generated.

**189**
On the other hand, a pool which normally has lifeguards present, may not need them when hired by a club whose members are all strong swimmers, or clubs where some of the members are qualified in lifesaving. When hiring a pool the general advice on hire to outside organisations, in paragraphs 183 and 184 and Appendix 5, should also be followed.

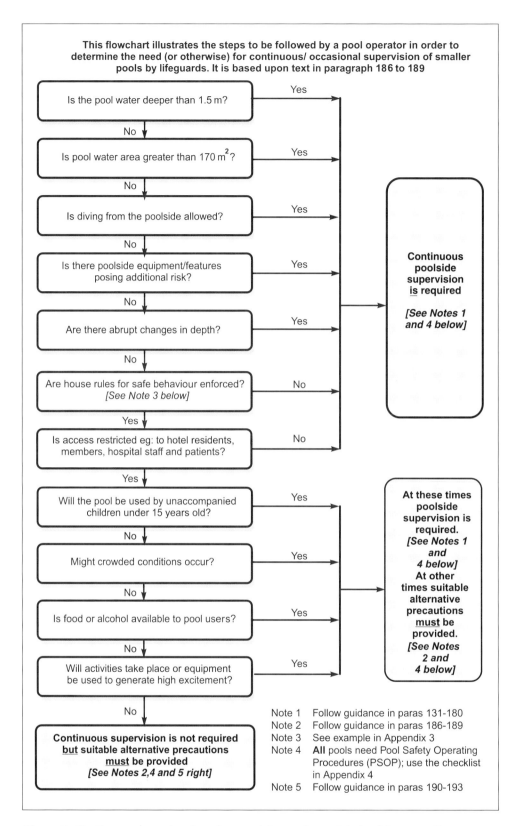

This flowchart illustrates the steps to be followed by a pool operator in order to determine the need (or otherwise) for continuous/ occasional supervision of smaller pools by lifeguards. It is based upon text in paragraph 186 to 189

Is the pool water deeper than 1.5 m? — No
Yes →

Is pool water area greater than 170 m² ? — No
Yes →

Is diving from the poolside allowed? — No
Yes →

Is there poolside equipment/features posing additional risk? — No
Yes →

Are there abrupt changes in depth? — No
Yes →

Are house rules for safe behaviour enforced? *[See Note 3 below]* — Yes
No →

**Continuous poolside supervision is required**

**[See Notes 1 and 4 below]**

Is access restricted eg: to hotel residents, members, hospital staff and patients? — Yes
No →

Will the pool be used by unaccompanied children under 15 years old? — No
Yes →

Might crowded conditions occur? — No
Yes →

Is food or alcohol available to pool users? — No
Yes →

Will activities take place or equipment be used to generate high excitement? — No
Yes →

**At these times poolside supervision is required. [See Notes 1 and 4 below] At other times suitable alternative precautions must be provided. [See Notes 2 and 4 below]**

**Continuous supervision is not required but suitable alternative precautions must be provided [See Notes 2,4 and 5 right]**

Note 1   Follow guidance in paras 131-180
Note 2   Follow guidance in paras 186-189
Note 3   See example in Appendix 3
Note 4   **All** pools need Pool Safety Operating Procedures (PSOP); use the checklist in Appendix 4
Note 5   Follow guidance in paras 190-193

**Figure 3**   Continuous/occasional pool supervision and associated safety precautions

**Precautions where constant poolside supervision is not provided**

*General safety procedures*

**190**   A clear, written safety procedure is particularly important where a pool may be used without constant poolside supervision. The procedure should be included in the PSOP, see paragraphs 47-53.

*Controlling access*

**191** Controlling access involves the following precautions:

- the number of bathers permitted to use the pool at any one time should be properly controlled and monitored (see paragraphs 202-206);
- where lone bathing is permitted, it is advisable to control entering and leaving so that pool operators know who is using the pool at any given time.

*Emergency arrangements*

**192** Where a risk assessment determines that a pool does not require constant poolside supervision, it is strongly recommended that the arrangements should include:

- signs at the entrance, in the changing rooms and in the pool area indicating that the pool is not staffed and drawing attention to simple rules of use and safety;
- signs in the pool area showing the depth of the water;
- an alarm to summon help in an emergency and a notice giving instruction in its use;
- suitable rescue equipment (poles, throwing ropes, buoyancy aids) available by the poolside, and clearly identifiable.

**193** Whenever the pool is in use, a member of staff will need to be designated as 'on call' to respond immediately to the alarm and deal with any emergency. It is essential that such staff are trained in pool rescue, CPR techniques and first aid.

**Violence**

**194** Employees whose job requires them to deal with the public can be at risk from violence. Swimming pools are largely for recreational use and are used by young people in particular. Spirited fun can sometimes lead to rowdy or boisterous groups of people, possibly resulting in an increased chance of aggravation or aggression towards staff or other pool users.

**195** Pool operators should manage the risk of violence in the same way as any other health and safety risk. Particular emphasis can be placed on training staff to 'spot' the early signs of aggression and either avoid it or cope with it. All employees should fully understand any backup systems, such as poolside alarms. Proper control and timely enforcement of 'house rules' are crucial to ensure the safe behaviour of both bathers and staff.

**196** Where there are particular problems it may also be necessary to consider physical security measures such as video cameras in identified areas of risk.

**197** Acts of violence towards staff resulting in injury are now required to be reported under RIDDOR.

**Controlling access to the pool**

*Preventing unauthorised access*

**198** Effective precautions (physical barriers, supervision, or both) should be taken to prevent unauthorised access to a pool intended to be out of use (eg closing time, while under repair). Children are often most at risk and special measures may need to be used. Plant rooms, chemical stores and other areas should be secured against unauthorised access. The risk assessment should include these factors.

**199** High walls or fences around an open-air pool may be an inadequate deterrent to prevent unauthorised use. The risks should be assessed and appropriate measures taken to reduce those risks, eg the installation of intruder lighting and/or alarms. Signs prohibiting unauthorised use should also be displayed.

### Pool covers

**200** Various types of pool cover are available, including simple hand-operated roller systems, automatically deployed covers, rising floors and decks and air-supported domes. Where pool covers are used as the primary means of preventing bathers' access (eg in some open-air pools which cannot be locked off after hours), the covers must be of a type which can be secured continuously around the edges. They must be capable of supporting the weight of any person walking or falling onto them and they should also be resistant to vandalism.

**201** Pool operators will need to ensure that their employees are not at risk from hazardous manual handling when dealing with this type of equipment (see paragraphs 28-32).

### Control of admissions

**202** Pool operators should, as part of the risk assessment, assess the maximum number of people who can safely be admitted to the pool or pool area and ensure that an effective method of control is in operation. Should there be a risk of the number being exceeded, admissions should be restricted.

**203** Admissions are normally controlled at the point of entry to the pool facility, rather than to the water itself, therefore allowance can be made in setting a maximum figure for the proportion of bathers likely to be out of the water at any one time. It is recommended therefore that operators, in determining maximum figures, set a standard of 3 m² per person for those in the water (for unprogrammed sessions) and base their figures using operational experience, taking into account all of the variables such as depth, size and shape. However, allowance should be made for any large influxes of bathers to the water particularly associated with the operation of equipment, such as wave machines.

**204** In addition to considerations of physical safety, the maximum loading should take account of the capacity of the pool water treatment plant and a control mechanism provided, such as a locker system, bands, keys or turnstiles to ensure that this figure is not exceeded.

**205** Pool operators will need to consider the number of young children (under the age of 8 years) allowed into the pool, during unprogrammed sessions, under the supervision of one parent or adult. The decision on whether or not to admit adults with parties of children should be made having followed the principles of risk assessment, taking into account the physical attributes of the pool tank, the pool environment, staffing levels, and where possible, the swimming capabilities of the children.

**206** Where groups of people with disabilities are using the pool, extra supervision may be required. For further information on supervising people with disabilities see the organisations listed in Appendix 7 and the publications listed in the Further reading section.

## Visibility

**207** A reduction in the clarity of the pool water is a risk to pool users. It is essential that bathers are able to assess the depth of the water and for lifeguards to see a casualty below the surface of the water. If the water clarity falls below a stated level (defined in the EAP), the EAP should identify the procedures for suspending admissions and clearing the pool until the clarity reaches an acceptable level (as a minimum, the ability to see the body of a small child if it were located on the floor of the pool in the deepest water). The clarity of the pool water should be constantly monitored.

**208** Glare can occur in both indoor pools (with large areas of glazing) and outdoor pools (effects of the weather). Reflection is a problem in indoor pools and may be caused by glazing or artificial lighting. Water features, such as waves, rapids, jets, or falling water, may produce turbulent water through which a lifeguard cannot see. Pool operators should identify these particular hazards as part of the risk assessment and include measures to reduce the risks.

## Emergency equipment and alarm systems

**209** Equipment provided for emergency use should be kept in its proper place, checked daily and maintained in good working order.

**210** All pools should have emergency equipment for use by lifeguards and others who may have supervisory responsibilities (eg swimming teachers, members of swimming clubs). Staff and other users should be trained in the use of the equipment, and it would be good practice to keep a record of the training. Pool operators will have identified the type of equipment required as part of the risk assessment, depending on the type and design of the pool, the user groups, etc.

**211** There may be a number of alarms for different types of emergencies, eg fire, plant failure, drowning, etc. Each alarm should be distinctive and it may help in buildings with a public address system to have recorded messages alerting staff to a particular type of emergency. All alarms should be tested daily and there should be a record of equipment and alarm checks.

## Child protection

**212** Pool operators have a duty of care to users of their premises; this will be greater in respect of children and will need to include the protection of children from abuse. Child abuse is a term used to describe ways in which children are harmed, usually by adults and often by people they know and trust. Anyone may have the potential to abuse children in some way and it is important that a pool operator takes all reasonable steps to ensure unsuitable people are prevented from working with children.

**213** When recruiting staff it is important that pool operators ask previous employers whether there are reasons for concern in relation to employing an individual whose duties will involve the supervision of children. A request for information should make it clear that the employment will involve supervising people under 18 years and that the information should include spent convictions. It is important that the references and past history of current employees as well as those applying for jobs are carefully checked.

**214** A pool operator, in asking for information on past convictions, can expect to receive information on criminal convictions even where they are spent. That is because employment concerned with the provision of leisure and recreational facilities to people aged under 18 years is exempt from the restrictions on disclosure of spent convictions in the Rehabilitation of Offenders Act 1974.

**215** In addition, pool operators will need to ensure there are effective systems in place to detect suspicious behaviour by adults in relation to children. The pool operator will need to:

- make all staff (whether paid or voluntary) aware of the problem of child abuse and to be alert to suspicious behaviour on the part of adults toward children and be aware of the possibility of misunderstanding leading to allegations of improper behaviour as a result of the relationship between staff and children;
- establish a procedure where staff who suspect actions by either users or other members of staff know who to refer the problem to;
- be aware of and control situations where overfriendliness of employees could lead to misconceived allegations;
- include awareness of these types of problems in the regular staff training programmes, in particular for those members of staff who supervise changing rooms;
- ensure that there are appropriate systems in place to monitor activities involving children (whether organised 'in-house' or by hirers of facilities). If there is any inappropriate behaviour, supervisory support and surveillance should be increased and/or the involvement of the police/social services should be sought.

**216** Further information and advice on protection of children is available - see Appendix 7 for a list of organisations and the Further reading section.

**Diving from the poolside**

**217** Pool operators will need to consider carefully the advisability of allowing diving from the poolside to take place during unprogrammed sessions. There are some pools where, because of a lack of water depth, a high freeboard or the pool floor profile, diving from the poolside should not be permitted.

**218** Pool operators will need to ensure that during unprogrammed sessions, diving is not permitted where it would be unsafe to do so and prohibition signs should be displayed to mark these areas of the pool. The minimum depth of water where shallow diving should be allowed is 1.5 m with a forward clearance of at least 7.6 m and freeboard height (pool surround above the water level) of no more that 0.38 m. The following types of diving should be prohibited in all areas of the pool during unprogrammed sessions:

- running dives;
- backward dives;
- dives without hands in front of head;

- indiscriminate diving;
- somersault entries;
- 'bombing'.

**219** In pools with a water depth of less than 1.5 m, all head-first entries and diving should be prohibited during unprogrammed sessions. (Further detailed advice can be sought from publications listed in the Reference and Further reading sections.)

## Safety of people with disabilities

**220** As part of the risk assessment, pool operators will need to consider people with disabilities on a case-by-case basis. They will need to ensure that:

- they consult with those they are trying to help;
- there are sufficient helpers in the water to provide support; and
- there are a sufficient number of other helpers, such as parents and friends, available to provide additional support and assistance. This is especially important in the event of an emergency requiring the evacuation of the building. Numbers will depend on the special needs of the people in the group;
- there are appropriate safety signs and signals (both visual and audible).

## Supervision of programmed sessions

**221** Programmed activities are those with a formal structure, ie disciplined, supervised or controlled and continuously monitored from the poolside. The more disciplined nature of such activities, with the presence of group or club organisers, may make it possible to reduce the number of lifeguards, particularly where the group or club has exclusive use of the pool.

**222** A particular example of 'programmed' swimming is where a public pool is used for swimming lessons conducted by a teacher employed by the school or local education authority. The pool operator will need to agree in advance with the organiser who will provide the necessary lifeguarding cover, and the numbers of lifeguards required (see also Appendix 5 on the arrangements for hiring the pool to outside organisations).

**223** The lifeguarding function can, in principle, be provided by the teacher or instructor with a class, provided they have a full range of lifeguarding skills (see paragraphs 165-167 for further information on teaching and coaching of programmed sessions, and Appendix 6 ). Where a class is divided into groups supervised by different teachers, whether it is sufficient for only one teacher to have full lifeguarding skills needs to be considered, according to all circumstances. In particular, the area and depth of water to be covered, the ages and swimming abilities of pupils, and the numbers being supervised, are all relevant. All those supervising should know and understand the relevant aspects of the PSOP.

**224** Where the pool is in shared use and clearly divided between programmed and unprogrammed swimming activities, suitably competent teachers and coaches may take responsibility (both for lifeguard cover and teaching and coaching) - but only for the programmed area of the pool. In addition they must work within the agreed ratio of pupils to teachers and coaches. Where the shared use is not clearly defined between programmed and unprogrammed activities, supervision must be provided in accordance with the pool's PSOP.

**225** Helpers and support teachers who do not have the necessary competences can play a valuable role in supporting those staff who do, in the safe delivery of programmed pool activities. The Reference and Further reading sections give details of available guidance which give further information.

### Supervision requirements for specialised activities

*Canoeing and sub-aqua*

**226** Lifeguards require specialised skills or additional knowledge to supervise canoeing and sub-aqua adequately. Organisations that can advise are listed in Appendix 7.

**227** When specialised equipment is being used, consideration will need to be given to protecting the pool finishes from damage, eg from heavy sub-aqua equipment cracking tiles or canoes eroding pool edges. Where there is a possibility of damage to the pool from the activity, appropriate preventative measures will need to be taken. When a pool has been used for specialised equipment and activities, its condition should be checked (eg for broken tiles) before bathers are readmitted.

*Social events*

**228** Social events, such as disco swimming, where high noise and excitement will be generated, will require particularly careful supervision. The risk assessment should take this into account and should be reflected in the length of duty spells of the lifeguards (see paragraphs 171-174).

*Consumption of food and drink*

**229** There should be specific supervision of areas where alcohol may be consumed, given both the possible effects on swimming ability and the risk of unruliness. It is strongly advised that activities in the water, eg children's pool parties, take place **before** food or drink are consumed, to avoid the increased risk of drowning.

### Equipment

**230** Where specialist equipment is provided, the operator will need to consider the risk and hazards stemming from its use and make arrangements for safe systems of work within the PSOP. The following are examples of the types of equipment which may be used:

- diving boards and platforms;
- water slides and flumes;
- river rides;
- wave machines;
- floating play equipment;
- inflatable structures;
- water features;
- spas;
- paddling pools.

### Supervision of equipment used by bathers

**231** The equipment, discussed in paragraphs 232-264, that is installed in the pool, should specifically be referred to in the risk assessment.  The risk control measures used by the pool operator should then be included in the NOP and EAP.

## Diving boards and platforms

**232** Diving boards should be directly supervised to ensure that they are used correctly and safely, and that swimmers and divers do not endanger each other.  Where equipment is positioned over an area of a main pool, some form of segregation on the surface of the water should be provided and additional supervision is likely to be required.

**233** Starting platforms should only be used under controlled conditions and under the supervision of correctly qualified staff.  They should be inspected prior to and at the end of use.  Where the removal of fixed platforms is not reasonably practicable or the pool has raised pool ends, this area of the pool should be carefully supervised to prevent unauthorised use (see paragraphs 217 - 219).

## Water slides

**234** The excitement of using a water slide may encourage bathers, particularly youngsters, to experiment in ways which add to the excitement, but can be extremely dangerous to themselves and others.  While the method of use will need to take into account the manufacturer's instructions it is known that the following kinds of behaviour may cause accidents:

- going down in pairs, or chains, or one rider too close to the next;
- riders stopping or slowing down (for example, this is possible when an open slide enters a covered section);
- standing up on the slide;
- going down head-first on slides not designed to be used in this way;
- failing to leave the landing pool immediately on arrival.

**235** Use and supervision arrangements for the slide should:

- take account of the manufacturer's instructions, eg on method of riding;
- include the display of suitable instructions and safety signs appropriately sited, including at the bottom of the stairway to the launch platform and the launch platform itself;
- include details for when the slide is in use so that the entry and landing points are supervised/controlled, and where there is a need for staff at both the entry and exit points, ensure good communication;
- take into account the control of entry so that riders are adequately spaced, and ensure communication between lifeguards.

**236** The lifeguard controlling the entry point should:

- ensure the body position of users is correct;
- control spacing of users;
- prevent 'chains' of users going down the slide together;
- prevent 'head-first' entry unless the ride is designed for it;
- stop users making a running start, thereby gaining excessive speed; and
- ensure there is orderly queuing.

**237** The lifeguard at the discharge point should:

- ensure that users move quickly out of the path of the slide;
- be particularly vigilant because users, especially children, may be disorientated and turbulence may make bathers difficult to see;
- arrange for any injuries to be attended to immediately, but without detracting from supervision.

**238** In certain circumstances, pool operators may wish to consider controlling the water slide by providing a traffic-light system at the top of the slide which utilises body movement sensors at the top and bottom of the slide path. The pool entry point should then be controlled by the pool lifeguard; however, depending on the design of the water slide, it may be better to have staff at the slide entry point.

**239** The slide will need to be inspected daily. Pool operators will need to ensure the necessary equipment is provided and a safe working practice is in place. Instructions in case of an accident or other emergency will need to be provided.

**240** When not in use, access to the slide will need to be prevented.

*Wave machines*

**241** A safe system of work will need to be devised for operating the wave mechanism. You may wish to consult the manufacturer about safe procedures and maintenance. The operator will need to consider:

- prior announcements requesting poor or non-swimmers to move to the beach area and swimmers to clear the immediate area in front of the wave machine (if necessary). This may be supplemented by audible and visual warnings, for example flashing lights;
- lifeguarding positions;
- intervals between successive operations;
- the effect of the waves on other features;
- ensuring that the machine can be switched off quickly and safely in an emergency;
- ensuring that the 'grilles' are designed to be safe (ie less than 100 mm between the grille bars).

**242** Those operating the equipment should have received instruction on switching off the machine safely in case of an emergency.

**243** Supervision will need to be from the sides, in order to see between the waves. Particularly careful vigilance will be required in view of the extra risks arising from:

- a large influx of bathers into the water, when the machine is to be operated;
- high excitement, and possible disorientation, especially among young children;
- bathers, particularly poor and non-swimmers and children, being struck by waves;
- jumping and diving while the wave machine is operating which is dangerous and should not be allowed.

**244** Bathers will need to be made aware, where appropriate, of different wave patterns and strengths and that the waves will make swimming more difficult.

## Inner-tube rides

**245** Where inner-tube rides are being used, consideration will need to be given to supervising the intermediate pool and the main splashdown area to ensure that bathers are not experiencing difficulty or are becoming trapped under the water and other bathers.

**246** Where inner-tube rides have been designed to produce a whirlpool effect in the intermediate pool, lifeguards will have to ensure that there is a steady movement of users and, where necessary, help forward motion. Those operating and supervising should be aware of the procedure in the event of an emergency evacuation.

## Slow and fast rivers

**247** Slow and fast rivers are a flat circuitous stream of water moved by booster pumps in which bathers float or swim.

**248** Pool operators will need to give consideration to:

- adequate monitoring of entry and exit points to prevent riders hitting walls or steps;
- adequate lifeguard numbers to visually cover the whole of the river path;
- pool steps, ladders and handrails which should be regularly checked for the tightness of bolts;
- the ease with which bathers can leave the stream of water;
- the procedure for cutting off/stopping the feature in an emergency.

## Falling rapids

**249** These involve riders descending an inclined channel in a fast-flowing stream of water. There may be intermediate pools with weirs at the start of separate sections of the channel.

**250** Pool operators will need to consider:

- supervision of bathers throughout the ride;
- positioning of lifeguards to provide observation of the complete ride, and to allow easy access in the event of an emergency;
- the control of the entry point, and of the flow of bathers in each section of the ride, to prevent congestion and an increased risk of injury by rider-to-rider impact;
- a procedure for rescuing panicking, injured or unconscious bathers.

**251** If the falling rapids are located outdoors, in whole or in part, lifeguards may need protection during adverse weather conditions, eg very hot or wet, etc. This should not hamper either their normal observation of the ride or their ability to intervene in any emergency.

## Inflatable play structures

**252** There are two general types of inflatable play structures, ie 'sealed' units which require inflating before use, and 'constant blow' units in which the air blower is in constant operation. Larger inflatables should be tethered to prevent them moving in the pool; the means of anchorage/tethering should not be a hazard to bathers. Prior to purchase, the suitability for use of the particular piece of equipment in a pool will need to be considered.

**253** Pool operators will need to assess the risks associated with using this type of equipment and give particular attention to the following points:

- its positioning, so that bathers cannot fall from it onto the pool edge;
- the siting to ensure there is an adequate depth of water should a bather dive or fall from the structure. If the inflatable is not a floating structure, eg takes the form of a water slide, pool operators will need to consider access and depth of water into which it discharges;
- adequacy of the anchorage points in the pool surround and in the inflatable itself, and that they are of suitable strength;
- if an electric blower is used, whether it is suitable in wet situations;
- whether the pool electrical installation and its protective systems are adequate and in accordance with the Electricity at Work Regulations 1989;
- the need for additional supervision, given that inflatables restrict vision through the water, including bathers directly under the inflatable, and that they encourage bathers to congregate in a small area;
- the risk of entanglement; and
- underwater lights may be helpful in ensuring that any bather underneath the equipment can be seen.

### Rafts and smaller inflatable toys

**254** This type of equipment poses many of the problems associated with the larger inflatables, including:

- falling against the poolside;
- lack of vision under the raft; and
- boisterous behaviour.

Additionally, because this type of equipment is often provided for the less able swimmer, there is a need to ensure that rafts and toys are kept in shallow water.

### Movable floors and bulkheads

**255** The provision of movable floors and bulkheads is an additional problem to consider when providing supervision of the pool. Pool operators will need to consider how the use of these features complicates sight lines, the difficulties where steep changes in level occur, and the procedures for lowering floors or moving bulkheads.

**256** The pool operator will need to include the detailed supervision requirements for the various alternative settings of the bulkheads and movable floors, highlighting any hazards which need to be considered, including the need for additional ladders in the pool.

## Pool hoists for those with disabilities

257 The use of both mobile and fixed electric/mechanical hoists can substantially reduce the need for manual handling.

258 Pool operators will need to:

- ensure that staff are fully trained in the use of the equipment;
- ensure that if slings are used instead of a seat or stretcher then 'dog-clips' are used to prevent the sling floating free from the supporting arm while in the water;
- ensure the capabilities of the individual are taken into consideration;
- ensure that the equipment is inspected and, if necessary, tested periodically by a competent person to ensure that the hoist can continue to safely lift loads up to its marked safe working load.

## Spas

259 Although spas are often operated as a popular 'add-on' feature to a swimming pool, they should **not** be considered simply as small swimming pools. Pool operators should have a thorough understanding of the technical operational requirements of a spa and be aware of the risks of incorrect operation. Relevant training will be required to provide pool operators with the necessary knowledge to effectively operate spa pools. Appendix 7 lists national bodies that can give advice on relevant training.

260 Individual supervision may not be necessary, depending on the siting of the spa pool, but the operator will need to consider a system of regular checks.

261 Signs should be displayed adjacent to the spa, advising on who should use the facility and how it should be used. The signs should include matters relating to age, medical condition of the user, duration of immersion and danger factors.

262 Means of summoning assistance in an emergency should be provided and the EAP should include details about emergencies within the spa pool.

263 Pool operators must assess the possible risk from micro-organisms and take suitable measures such as regular chemical and microbiological testing as well as regular checks on the correct operation of disinfectant and filtration plant.

## Paddling pools

264 Where a paddling pool is provided as part of a swimming facility, it should be included within the PSOP for the building. Where a paddling pool is provided separately, such as in a park, there will be a need to consider the arrangements for its safe operation and these should include:

- daily routines for cleaning and inspection;
- provision of signs governing its use and carer responsibility;
- provision of signs relating to unsafe situations and emergencies.

# General maintenance - plant and equipment

## Introduction

**265** Regular and correct maintenance of buildings, plant and equipment is important in ensuring the health and safety of employees and pool users. The designer's (or manufacturer's) instructions should preferably specify the preventive maintenance procedures and intervals. They should also indicate the competence and/or qualifications for those carrying out the work. Where divers are used for installing, maintaining, repairing or cleaning of swimming pools, the requirements of the Diving at Work Regulations 1997 should be followed. If suitable specifications are not available from designers or manufacturers, operators should draw up their own, and include them as part of the normal operating procedure.

**266** Manufacturer's instructions on operation of plant and equipment should be made conveniently available to attendants, eg by attaching copies to the plant itself.

**267** Pool operators should ensure that inspections and tests are carried out at the specified intervals as a preventative measure, and any remedial action that is required is promptly dealt with.

**Protecting the public during maintenance activities, etc**

**268** Suitable precautions should be taken to protect the public who may be present during maintenance/work activities. It is recommended in paragraphs 198-199 that effective measures should be taken to prevent unauthorised public access to a pool intended to be out of use. Particular consideration is needed where the public may have access - unauthorised or otherwise - alongside a pool which is empty, or at a reduced depth. Pool operators should consider who may be at risk, and the possible need for edge protection.

**Cleanliness**

**269** Pool operators need to ensure that:

- floors and stairs are kept clean, are drained where necessary, and are not slippery;
- the premises are kept clean, including internal walls, ceilings, furniture and fittings;
- appropriate containers are provided for waste material;
- refuse and trade waste are disposed of regularly; and
- spillages are promptly cleared up.

**Heating, ventilation and air-conditioning systems**

**270** These systems need to be considered together. High temperature, poor humidity control and inadequate ventilation or air distribution can be major factors in any potential deterioration of the pool structure and finishes, and can increase risks associated with electrical fittings. The concentration and efficiency of pool staff, and users' safety, can also be affected.

**271** A safe environment depends on good standards of design and installation of systems and equipment. When new installations are commissioned they should be assessed to ensure that they meet the original design specification.

**272** The requirements for the design, construction, installation and operation of pressure equipment, used for example in the pool's heating system, are covered by the Pressure Systems and Transportable Gas Containers Regulations 1989.

**273** A written scheme of examination, which has been approved by a competent person, must be prepared before a system can be operated. The Regulations also require that the system is properly maintained in good repair, to prevent accidents and incidents.

**274** The swimming pool hall, changing rooms and other occupied areas should be maintained at a comfortable temperature and have an adequate number of air changes per hour. A temperature of around 27 ˚C - 29.5 ˚C for the water, with the air temperature about 1 ˚C higher, may be most suitable; this will help to avoid excess condensation. (Where significantly higher temperatures are maintained, for example in some leisure or learner pools, possible adverse effects on lifeguards' capacity to remain alert for long periods will need to be taken into account as part of the risk assessment and when deciding on maximum duty spells, see paragraphs 171-174).

**275** Where, for heat recovery purposes, ventilation air is recirculated, care must be taken to ensure there is not a build-up of harmful compounds in the pool hall air; a minimum of 30% fresh air should be provided.

**276** Changing areas should be maintained at a temperature of 24 °C and have ten air changes per hour to avoid condensation, and ancillary areas at about 20 °C. Recommendations for pool water and air temperatures are published in the *Handbook of sports and recreational building design*,[9] available from Sport England Publications. Care should be taken with ventilation to avoid draughts.

## Safe working practices

**277** Pool operators should ensure that:

- pipework is lagged if it is likely to become hot enough to cause injury (may not apply if pipes are at a high level);
- where necessary, pipelines are marked either with warning signs or labels in accordance with the Health and Safety (Safety Signs and Signals) Regulations 1996. Whether this needs to take place will be decided by the risk assessment. If the risk is not significant, there is no need to provide a sign. If the contents of the pipelines change regularly, there is no need to mark them, provided other equally effective measures are in place to protect employees;
- employees do not enter a confined space because of the risk of serious injury, eg being overcome by gases, fumes, etc. Entry to a confined space should be carefully controlled under a safe system of work in accordance with the Confined Spaces Regulations 1997;
- they carry out a study to identify if any asbestos is present, eg the boiler house, etc, in accordance with *Managing asbestos in workplace buildings*.[14] Where there is a possibility that employees may work with asbestos, the risk assessment should identify the types of asbestos, the nature and degree of exposure, and the steps to be taken to prevent or reduce exposure to the lowest reasonably practicable level;
- any work with asbestos insulation or asbestos coating should be carried out, with few exceptions, by people licensed by HSE under the Asbestos (Licensing) Regulations 1983. HSE may have to be notified in advance, either as a licence condition or if an employer's own employees are to undertake the work. All work with asbestos is subject to the Control of Asbestos at Work Regulations 1987 (associated with the Regulations are two Approved Codes of Practice);
- contractors are working in accordance with the Regulations and Codes of Practice to prevent exposure and release of asbestos fibres from the workplace.

## Maintenance

**278** Where bunded fuel storage tanks are situated in the open air, rainwater collected in the bund should preferably be pumped out over the bund walls.

**279** Storage vessels and delivery pipeline systems for liquefied petroleum gas (LPG) should be installed and maintained in accordance with HSE booklet *Storage of LPG at fixed installations*.[15]

### Examination and inspection

**280** Boilers should be thoroughly examined/re-examined:

- after dismantling, when cold;
- while operating, under normal conditions;
- after any substantial repair.

**281** After each examination a report should be obtained and kept available for inspection.

**282** Ventilation systems should be inspected every three months. Filter units should be cleaned as part of the general maintenance procedures. Effectiveness of the system should be monitored at least annually.

### Ventilation

**283** Effective and suitable ventilation should be provided throughout the building by a sufficient quantity of fresh or purified air. This can be achieved by means of mechanical ventilation or air-conditioning systems.

**284** Where necessary, for reasons of health and safety, ventilation equipment should be fitted with audible or visual warning of any failure of the ventilation system.

**285** Careful consideration should be given to any air recirculation system where pool hall air is to be used because recirculation of contaminants could increase overall contamination levels. Further advice is available in the *Workplace (Health, Safety and Welfare) Regulations 1992 Approved Code of Practice*.[16]

### Lighting

**286** Suitable and sufficient lighting should be provided (by the use of natural light) so far as is reasonably practicable and maintained throughout the building. Further advice can be obtained from the *Workplace (Health, Safety and Welfare) Regulations 1992 Approved Code of Practice*[16] and guidance in *Lighting at work*[17] issued by HSE.

**287** Automatic emergency lighting, powered by an independent source, should be provided where sudden loss of light would create a risk, eg during a power failure, so that emergency evacuation procedures can be carried out safely.

### Glazing

**288** Glazing, including windows in transparent or translucent surfaces in walls, partitions, light fittings, doors and gates should, where necessary for reasons of health and safety, be made of safety material or be protected against breakage. Examples of safety material are:

- polycarbonates or glass blocks; or
- toughened, laminated glass or safety wire glass, which if it breaks, breaks safely, ie breaks in a way that does not result in large sharp pieces; or
- ordinary annealed glass which meets the following thickness criteria:

| Nominal thickness | Maximum size |
| --- | --- |
| 8 mm | 1.1 m x 1.1 m |
| 10 mm | 2.25 m x 2.25 m |
| 12 mm | 3 m x 4.5 m |
| 15 mm | Any size |

289  If there is a danger of people coming into contact with glass, it should be marked, or the pool operator should incorporate features to make it apparent. Pool operators will need to consider, as part of the risk assessment, whether there is a foreseeable risk of people being injured either by direct contact with glazing, or as a result of the glazing being broken. If so, the glazing will need to meet the requirements of regulation 14 of the Workplace (Health, Safety and Welfare) Regulations to ensure it is protected in some way.

*Maintenance*

290  To ensure that the standard of lighting is maintained:

■ external windows should be kept clean;

■ artificial lighting should be maintained in good working order, with units kept clean (where appropriate), and a provision made for replacement if a defect causes illumination to fall below a safe level at which a view of the pool bottom is impaired;

■ emergency lighting should be tested daily;

■ illumination values should be checked annually to ensure there is no deterioration.

291  Access for cleaning windows and light fittings poses some special problems in addition to the general problems associated with working at heights. Further guidance published by HSE is available in regulation 16 of the *Workplace (Health, Safety and Welfare) Regulations 1992 Approved Code of Practice*.[16]

292  Where work is required above fragile ceilings, roofs or roof lights, suitable walkways and platforms should be provided. These should:

■ be of adequate dimensions and strength, and properly supported;

■ have suitable edge protection (toe boards, handrails and mid-rails) as required;

■ take the employee close enough to the work to avoid any risk of overbalancing.

292  Precautions should be taken to prevent any articles being dropped, eg through fragile materials onto people below. Therefore tools should be secured or tethered whenever possible.

**Electrical installations and equipment**

294  The various risks from electricity - injury from mechanical movement of electronically activated equipment, burns and fire - are magnified by the wet and

corrosive conditions in pools and associated areas. Pool operators need to be aware of the various risks, and take appropriate precautions. The Electricity at Work Regulations 1989 set out the legal requirements for safe electrical installations, equipment and safe working practices.

**295** Work on electrical installations and equipment requires specialist knowledge and skills. It should only be undertaken or supervised by those who possess the appropriate knowledge or experience to ensure the work is done safely.

*Electrical installation*

**296** Fixed electrical installations and any subsequent alterations, extensions and repairs should be to a suitable standard, such as *Requirements for electrical installations* BS 7671:1992[12] (also known as the Institution of Electrical Engineers (IEE) Wiring Regulations, though these Regulations are not in fact statutory duties). BS 7671:1992[12] sets out, among other things, the types of electrical systems suitable for different locations within the pool complex, the application of measures against electric shock, and the types of switchgear and accessories that may be suitable.

**297** The responsibility for ensuring that the electrical installation is effectively earthed and bonded where necessary, rests with the pool operator. The integrity and effectiveness of the earthing and bonding needs to be verified by inspection and tested annually. Pool operators may need to seek specialist advice on this.

**298** Where possible, switches should be fitted to enable parts of the installation to be disconnected from the supply. These switches should be of the type designed to provide electrical isolation so that maintenance, modification and/or repair can be undertaken safely.

**299** Socket outlets should not normally be located in wet areas. Where they are, they should be of a type suitable for that environment, in accordance with EN 60309-2:1998[18] (formerly known as BS 4343). Particular care should be taken where hoses or water jets are used.

**300** The supply to these outlets, and those used to supply leads and equipment to be used in wet areas, should be protected to reduce risk from electric shock. This can be either by the use of earth monitoring systems (particularly for 415 V ac supplies) or supplies fed via non-adjustable residual current devices (RCDs) with a rated tripping current not exceeding 30 mA. Pool operators may need specialist advice regarding installation of RCDs.

**301** RCDs should be:

- installed in a damp-proof enclosure (the test button and reset button should be accessible but exclude the ingress of damp) and all cable entries should be properly sealed (see the manufacturer's instructions);
- protected against mechanical damage and vibration;
- checked daily by operating the test button;
- inspected weekly, together with the equipment it is supplying, during the formal visual inspection;
- tested every three months by an electrician using appropriate electrical test equipment.

**302** The tests should not be carried out on RCDs at a time when loss of power may adversely affect other work activities or the public in the complex.

**Potentially flammable atmospheres**

**303** It is unlikely that the creation of an explosive atmosphere will occur in any chemical treatment area. However, if electrical equipment is to be used in an area where an explosive atmosphere could occur, eg adjacent to an electrolytic sodium hypochlorite generator which produces hydrogen as a by-product, or where there is a possibility of an explosive dust cloud, it should be suitable for such use. Guidance as to the selection and installation of suitable equipment can be found in BS 5345:1989[19] (superseded by BS EN 60079-14:1997) and BS 6941:1988.[20]

*Portable electrical equipment*

**304** Electrical equipment should not normally be used in wet areas. Where it is necessary to use portable electrical equipment at or near the poolside, it must be selected and used carefully to reduce the electrical risks. The use of certain types of equipment will eliminate, or reduce substantially, these electrical risks, for example:

- air-powered tools;
- equipment designed to withstand immersion in water;
- battery-operated tools;
- 25 V waterproof portable hand lamps (IP56 or IP57, or IPX6 or IPX7);
- 50 V tools fed from a safe extra low voltage (SELV) system;
- 110 V tools fed from a reduced low voltage (RLV) system. This is usually an isolating transformer (see BS 3535:1990)[21] that is centre tapped to earth on the secondary output winding.

**305** A voltage as low as 50 V can be fatal to someone immersed in the water, so pool operators should consider fitting electrically powered equipment used on or adjacent to the pool or over the pool, with restraints or erecting barriers to stop it falling into the water.

**306** Mains voltage audio and similar equipment should not be allowed on or near the side of the pool unless it was specifically designed for use in or around water. Pool operators should ensure that third parties, eg aqua aerobics coaches, do not bring unsuitable electrical items on to the poolside. Electrical equipment not designed for use in or around water should be located in a dry room away from the pool and where possible equipment such as loudspeakers and electronic clocks should be situated out of reach of pool users and water. In addition, they should be connected by permanently installed cabling with proper connection facilities. If it is necessary to use temporary installations during non-programmed sessions, equipment and cabling should be situated out of reach of the pool users.

*Maintenance*

**307** The electrical installations and associated equipment should be maintained in a safe condition. Planned routine maintenance, user checks and servicing in line with the manufacturer's instructions will all help achieve this.

**308** The fixed electrical installation should be periodically inspected and tested at intervals appropriate to its age and condition. Guidance is given in Guidance Note 3 *Inspection and testing* to BS 7671: 1992[12] (the 16th edition of the Institution of Electrical Engineers (IEE) Wiring Regulations). Circuits or apparatus which are not satisfactory should be disconnected from the supply and removed from service. They should be repaired (or replaced) and tested before they are put back into service.

**309** In a wet or humid environment, the risks from damaged or faulty portable electrical equipment are high, and need managing and controlling by an appropriate maintenance system. HSE's booklet *Maintaining portable and transportable electrical equipment*[22] gives general advice on the electrical safety aspects of maintaining portable and transportable equipment.

**310** The frequency of inspection is dependent on the type of equipment and how it is used. Cost-effective maintenance can be achieved by establishing a programme combining checks by the user, formal visual inspections on a regular basis and combined inspection and testing where necessary. The following advice explains what is meant by each of these forms of inspection.

### User checks

The person using the equipment should be encouraged, after basic training, to visually check the electrical equipment they use for signs that it is not in a safe condition. The user should not attempt to dismantle the equipment or plug.

### Formal visual inspection

To control the risk and monitor the user checks, a competent person (ie someone who has received adequate training) should carry out regular formal inspections which include visual checks undertaken in a systematic way. Additional checks should include: the removal of plug covers; checking that a proper fuse is correctly fitted; checking connections to ensure they are secure and checking for evidence of overheating (burn marks or discoloration).

### Combined inspection and testing

Electrical testing can detect faults such as loss of earth continuity, deterioration of the insulation and internal or external contamination by dust, water, etc. These faults may not be picked up by user checks or formal visual inspections. It is therefore important that combined inspection and testing is carried out by a person trained to do so at intervals appropriate to the type of equipment and the risks. In addition to routine testing as part of the planned maintenance programme, combined inspection and testing is also recommended if there is reason to suspect the equipment may be faulty, damaged or contaminated. This is especially important where these faults cannot be confirmed by visual inspection; or after any repair, modification or similar work to the equipment; or when its integrity needs to be established.

**311** The most important precaution is the formal visual inspection because this can detect about 95% of faults or damage. Pool operators should ensure that regular visual inspections are carried out by competent members of staff. Such staff need:

- sufficient training to enable them to detect signs of faults or damage;
- time to enable them to carry out the inspections properly.

**312** Unsafe electrical equipment should be taken out of use in such a way that it cannot accidentally re-enter service before it has been repaired or replaced.

**313** It is strongly recommended that records are checked to keep track of and review the maintenance procedures.

# The pool water treatment system

## Introduction

 This section gives guidance on how disinfection and other treatment systems, filtration and circulation of pool water (including arrangements for the storage and handling of chemicals) should be operated to ensure the safety of pool users and employees. Water treatment systems are a critical part of the architectural and mechanical design, involving issues like bathing load and turnover. These issues are dealt with in more detail in the guidance published by the Pool Water Treatment Advisory Group (PWTAG).

## Safe working practices

 Many of the systems and processes described in this section involve potentially dangerous chemicals. The written safety policy should include management's assessment of hazards associated with all aspects of operation of the plant, and precautions to control the risk.

 The main hazards associated with pool water treatment systems include:

- risks to bathers or employees from chemicals used in disinfecting systems. These include: irritation of skin, eyes and the respiratory system by disinfectants and disinfection by-products; infection; the possibility of fire due to some disinfectants being strong oxidising agents; and leaks of toxic gases. The most serious risks are of the uncontrolled escape of chlorine gas, eg following inadvertent mixing of a chlorine-based disinfectant with acids, and of accidents, even explosions;

■ unclear, opaque or cloudy water may present a risk to bathers and may indicate that the quality is unacceptable due to inadequate water treatment or may result from bather overload;

■ miscellaneous risks to employees, for example from working in confined spaces, use of electrical equipment, etc;

■ risks to bathers from poor hydraulic design, eg inlets and outlets of unsafe design and operating at pressures where suction from outlets or the buffeting from inlets can result in a hazard to bathers.

**Control of Substances Hazardous to Health (COSHH) Regulations 1994**

**317** Under the COSHH Regulations every employer has a responsibility to assess the risks associated with hazardous substances in the workplace and to take adequate steps to eliminate or control those risks. This applies to all substances that can adversely affect health, including those listed as toxic, harmful, irritant or corrosive under the Chemicals (Hazard, Information and Packaging for Supply) Regulations 1994. These Regulations cover the majority of swimming pool chemicals, hence the need for special care when choosing and using such materials. The Regulations also cover the risks arising from micro-organisms.

**318** A five-step approach is recommended when undertaking a COSHH and management assessment.

**Step 1**
Read all the available advice, including instructions and manuals from the equipment suppliers, labels, safety material, data sheets and instruction booklets from chemical suppliers, and this guidance.

**Step 2**
Do the COSHH and management assessments, and generate work procedures, keeping the procedures simple and easy to understand, and including NOPs, signs, labels, locks, records, etc.

**Step 3**
If the assessments suggest relatively easy improvements to safety, put them into operation. If the necessary precautions are very complex, try to change the conditions that make all the precautions necessary.

**Step 4**
Make a record of the assessment unless it could easily be repeated and explained at any time because it is simple and obvious, or the work is straightforward and low risk and the time taken to record it is disproportionate.

**Step 5**
Consider if and when the assessment is to be reviewed.

A full *Step-by-step guide to COSHH assessment*[23] is available from HSE Books.

## Assessment

**319** The first step is for the employer to assess the risk of each chemical. This must be carried out by a competent person - perhaps a member of the management team for a small, stand-alone pool, or often a specialist team in a multi-function local authority department. This process will also need to call on the experience and knowledge of others, for example the assessor will need to know about:

- which chemicals are used and how they are used (including storage);
- other chemicals on site - by reference to material safety data sheets, etc;
- site location in relation to the impact of a chemical accident;
- staff training and competence in using chemicals;
- risks to health arising from micro-organisms.

**320** Where this assessment is carried out under COSHH, there is no need for further assessment to comply with the Management of Health and Safety at Work Regulations 1992, provided the assessment is regularly reviewed and remains valid.

## Risk control

**321** The next step under COSHH is to prevent or control exposure to hazardous substances. Prevention is obviously best. The pool operator will need to consider whether this can be achieved by substituting a less harmful substance, or one that is compatible with other chemicals on site. This may reduce the risk to health due to fire, explosion or the production of toxic gases.

**322** Only where prevention is not reasonably practicable can the pool operator turn to other controls. Personal protective equipment should not be the first option. Instead, the risk must be reduced to acceptable limits by 'engineering' control measures such as using the least potentially harmful chemical that can achieve the purpose intended effectively and efficiently and by isolating or physically separating chemicals. These procedures must be systematically recorded to include:

- identification of the hazards;
- identification of who might be harmed and how;
- evaluation of the risks arising from the hazards, and decisions about precautions;
- recording the findings;
- regular review of the assessments and any necessary revisions.

**323** The COSHH Regulations require suppliers of chemicals to provide a material safety data sheet (MSDS) for each chemical. It is also the installer's responsibility to provide relevant information on plant safety, etc - which may include MSDSs. There will need to be MSDSs for all the chemicals in the plant room including test reagent chemicals, cleaning chemicals, chemicals used in maintenance programmes, etc.

## Training

**324** The COSHH Regulations require that staff involved in the handling and use of chemicals should receive appropriate training and instruction. Even the most thorough arrangements to comply with the COSHH Regulations will fail unless all employees are aware of the risks associated with their work and how these risks can be avoided. (See Appendix 7 for training providers).

**325** **Only competent people should handle chemicals**. Training will need to include sufficient knowledge and understanding of the chemicals for staff to be alert to any changes affecting safety. Staff must be trained in, and the clear written procedures should be distributed to all employees involved in, the operation of plant or the handling of chemicals. The written procedures will need to include:

- safety requirements;
- labelling and safety notices;
- MSDSs (maintained on site) for all chemicals used;
- information on delivery, storage, handling and use.

**326** The training for the safe operation and use of equipment and chemicals will need to:

- be related specifically to the operation and maintenance of the particular plant, hazards associated with it, and substances used. Employees' attention should be drawn to any manufacturers' instructions, and copies made conveniently available (eg secured to the plant itself);
- be given to enough employees to ensure that plant need never be operated by untrained staff;
- include pool managers, to ensure they understand the functioning of the pool water system, including the plant and associated hazards, sufficiently to supervise safe operation;
- include the use, care and maintenance of personal protective equipment;
- require those who have been trained, to demonstrate that they can operate and maintain the plant safely.

**327** Pool operators will need to check that staff understand and follow all procedures and responsibilities. Monitoring and review of the effectiveness of arrangements should then follow. Details of actual training sessions will need to be recorded and reviewed. Information, instruction, and training are the essential requirements for all staff involved in the storage, handling, and use of swimming pool chemicals.

**Personal protective equipment**

**328** The Personal Protective Equipment Regulations 1992 require pool operators to assess and provide necessary personal protective equipment (PPE) when performing certain tasks. It is recommended that pool operators take the advice of suppliers of equipment and chemicals as to what PPE are needed. Some or all of the following protective clothing may be needed during delivery, handling of materials, cleaning or maintenance:

- dust masks and face protection;
- eye protection (to British Standard EN 166:1996)[24];
- aprons or chemical suits;
- boots;
- gauntlets;
- respirators.

*Respirators*

**329** Where chlorine gas or liquid bromine are used, or there is any risk of generating chlorine or bromine gas by accidental mixing of chemicals, it is particularly important to provide precautions against exposure to toxic gases. Sufficient canister respirators for all employees liable to be present at any one time should be kept available in or near plant rooms. Canister respirators should be located in the immediate area where the leak may occur and also at the entrance door to these areas where they can be used by staff who may have to go into the area where a leak is apparent.

**330** Employees who have to work with the chemicals should have respirators on personal issue. The type of respirator, training, instructions and maintenance arrangements should be determined as part of the assessments.

**331** Canister respirators can only deal with low concentrations of toxic gases. Pool operators need to consider suitable emergency procedures for more serious leaks, where appropriate in consultation with the fire authorities.

**332** Canister respirators should only be used as a last resort. Where they are used, it is important that attention be paid to the manufacturer's instructions, in particular the limitations of the product, and that canisters are replaced shortly after the seal has been broken.

**Delivery, storage and handling of chemicals**

**333** Advice on delivery, storage and handling of chemicals is given in a PWTAG publication *Swimming pool water - treatment and quality control*.[13] The principles and advice given can, in some cases, also be applied to small systems using small quantities of materials.

**334** Chemicals should be kept only in the containers in which they were received from the suppliers, or containers intended for that purpose and correctly marked with the safety information and product identity. The pool operator has a duty to use suitably marked containers that have been specifically designed to hold chemicals. Temporary unlabelled containers should not be used.

**335** Suitably designed trolleys or similar equipment should be used to transport cylinders and heavy drums, which should be kept upright. It is strongly advised against rolling or dragging the containers. The transfer, whether by lifting or not, of materials into a bunded area needs care (see HSE's *Manual handling. Manual Handling Operations Regulations 1992*,[25] and *Manual handling: Solutions you can handle*)[26]. Materials should not be transferred into containers not designed for that purpose. Empty containers should not be left on site or used for other purposes but be disposed of as soon as possible.

*Delivery on site*

**336** When chemicals are to be delivered, sufficient space for parking and manoeuvring should be provided close to the storage area. Precautions (eg supervision, warning signs, or barriers) should be taken as necessary to protect the public or employees who may have access to the delivery area. Materials should be moved into storage as soon as possible, and never left unattended in a public area.

**337** For bulk deliveries, a written delivery procedure should be agreed with the supplier, in accordance with hazard data sheets. Incompatible materials (eg acid and alkali), if delivered in the same vehicle, should be effectively segregated. Where sodium hypochlorite is delivered from a tanker to a day tank, the pipework, and connections, should be specific to that delivery, to prevent delivery hoses being incorrectly connected up. Loading points should be clearly labelled.

*Storage*

**338** Storage rooms should:

- be clearly marked, warning of the possible danger, and be secure locations accessible only by authorised employees;
- not be plant rooms unless the chemicals carry no risk of fire and are contained in bunds of suitable design, as outlined in paragraph 341;
- be at the same level as the delivery point and accessed directly from outside (ideally by ramp rather than steps). This will assist ventilation, and movement of materials (including in an emergency);
- not be situated close to public areas, doors, windows or ventilation intakes. This reduces the risk of any release of toxic fumes being drawn into the building;
- have adequate natural ventilation to the open air in a safe position (ie not to a public area, or to a place from where fumes may enter the building). If adequate natural ventilation is not reasonably practicable, mechanical ventilation should be provided. Where failure of ventilation would pose a serious hazard (eg for a chlorine gas store), a flow switch should be incorporated in any mechanical system to sound an alarm in case of fan breakdown. However, chlorine gas is safest when stored in a specially designed sealed room that in case of a major leakage from a cylinder prevents the gas from escaping (see paragraphs 377-378);
- provide clean and dry storage for solid materials (raised on pallets or stilts to avoid contact with any water which may enter the store);
- protect containers from direct sunlight, and isolate them from hot pipework or plant.

**339** In addition, it is important that storage rooms also provide enclosures with a minimum of half an hour fire resistance for all chemicals, in view of risks from over-heating, such as:

- fire;
- dangerous fumes being given off;
- leakage from damaged plastic containers;
- explosion of pressurised containers.

**340** Different types of chemicals should be effectively segregated in storage and use. This is particularly important where different disinfectants, or acids and disinfectants, may come into contact with each other and produce chlorine gas, fire or an explosion.

**341** Each liquid chemical, whether in tanks or drums, should be in a separate bund; each bund should be capable of holding 110% of the chemical stored. Bunds must allow for puncture of the drums or tanks. Bunded areas should be clearly marked, giving details of the contents.

### Handling of chemicals

**342** Employees will need protection against some chemicals. The risk assessment must take this into consideration and determine the most appropriate protection to be used. Safe systems of work should be followed to protect employees from contacting, ingesting or inhaling harmful materials. For example: conditions for weighing and mixing materials should be carefully controlled and protective equipment supplied, mixing areas must be ventilated, and local exhaust ventilation will need to be considered.

**343** Smoking should be prohibited when handling chemicals.

### Hazards associated with the disinfection system

#### *Hypochlorite and acid systems*

**344** Pool water treatment systems that dose the pool water, either automatically or manually controlled, with either calcium or sodium hypochlorite and acid, have on occasions resulted in the release of chlorine gas into the atmosphere. Most incidents have occurred when water circulation has stopped or been reduced but the automatic dosing system has continued to operate. This produces a build-up of hypochlorite and acid which react together to produce chlorine gas. The gas is then discharged into the pool hall when water circulation is restored. This possibility should be taken into account in the EAP.

**345** The loss of water circulation or reduced flow can be caused by failure of the pumps, loss of prime, manual isolation of the pumps during maintenance, or the operation of bypass valves (which reduce water flow within the pipeline).

#### *Fail-safe systems*

**346** In all disinfecting systems which incorporate automatic chemical dosing (including those using chlorine, unless the chlorine injection system is negative pressure and the chlorine gas line has a vacuum-operated regulator), the following precautions should be considered as appropriate:

- interlocking the dosing system electrically with the water circulating pumps, to prevent the continuation of dosing, should the pumps fail;
- incorporating into the circulation system a fail-safe, flow measuring device capable of detecting a reduction or cessation of flow and interlocking this with the dosing pumps to prevent continuation of dosing;
- siting the pool water circulation pumps below the level of the pool water, to minimise the risk of the pumps losing their prime;
- locating an additional sampling point close to the chemical injection point for alarm purposes. (Automatic dosing systems operate by sampling the water and activating or stopping the dosing pumps as required, for example following a change in bather loads.) Disinfectant dosing should cut off when the system fails;
- siting the calcium/sodium hypochlorite and acid injection points as far apart as possible (preferably a minimum of 1 m); ideally the hypochlorite injection point should be located before the filter and the acid dosing point after the filter and heat exchanger;

- designing dosing lines so that they are protected from damage, and so that they cannot, inadvertently, be connected the wrong way round;
- displaying notices warning of the risks of mixing calcium/sodium hypochlorite and acids, and the importance of maintaining pool water circulation during dosing;
- ensuring that pressured chemicals in the line are safely relieved before breaking the delivery line for maintenance work to be carried out. Pipelines and injection points can become blocked by calcium deposit. Removal is usually carried out with acid; therefore the pipes will need to have been flushed out, the acid then added to descale, flushed out again and released for maintenance.

### Circulation feeder devices

**347** Circulation feeders are items of equipment that take dry chemicals and introduce them into the pool. They are mainly used for disinfectants, though they have some use in dosing pH chemicals. There are two types:

- erosion feeders are designed so that water flowing through them physically erodes material from a dry tablet; this subsequently dissolves in the water circulation. Calcium hypochlorite and trichlorinator feeders can be of this type;
- soaker feeders allow water to dissolve material from the tablet directly. Brominators are of this type.

**348** On most types of circulation feeder the water supply to the feeder is taken from the pressure side of the main circulation pumps and returns to the suction side of the pumps. The water passes through the feeder and is returned to the main circulation line. This has the advantage that it fails safe if the water circulation fails. Circulation feeders may be fitted with automatic controls, which will help to prevent overdosing.

**349** Circulation feeder devices should only be used for the purpose, and chemicals, for which they were designed. Calcium hypochlorite, chlorinated isocyanurates and bromochlorodimethylhydantoin (BCDMH) all have specific feeders and it is vitally important that they are only used for the chemical for which they are designed. Using the wrong chemical in a feeder can result in the formation of dangerous gases, fire or explosion. It is very important that chemicals are not mixed in closed containers/feeders as this may cause explosions. Any closed vessels used for feeding chemicals need to be safeguarded against pressure accumulation and should be fitted with a pressure relief valve. Circulation feeder devices should be emptied of chemicals if the pool circulation system is to be closed down for a period of time.

### Systems design

**350** The system design should take into account the possible sources of the hazards, which systems are important for safety, and the associated safety integrity of those systems. From this the reliability and quality of equipment can be obtained and an appropriate equipment configuration designed. This should be undertaken by those with appropriate knowledge and expertise in this area.

### Systems maintenance

**351** To prevent system failure, the equipment needs to be maintained to ensure it is functioning correctly and that its condition is not deteriorating. This can be achieved by regular testing of all warning and safety devices, the interlocks, and inspection of the equipment by a competent person. The required frequency of this testing depends on the system design and on the particular equipment installed. The manufacturer's advice should be followed. In the absence of this, all safety interlocks should be tested at three-monthly intervals.

### Disposal of wastes

As part of the water treatment process the pool operator should consult the relevant waste disposal authority about the disposal of wastes. The manufacturer's instructions concerning disposal of containers and materials should also be followed.

### Disinfectants and bacteriological water quality

In order to establish that the pool is without risks to the health of those using it, pool operators will need to ensure, under the COSHH Regulations, that they have adequately controlled the risks from exposure to micro-organisms. To do this, adequate disinfecting of the pool will need to take place and bacteriological sampling will be required.

Bacteriological sampling will need to be undertaken monthly in pools in use all year round. Constant checking of the correct disinfectant level and pH value will ensure the bacteriological quality of a well-run pool. Bacterial levels should be zero (or near zero) as a 'baseline'. More frequent samples will be necessary where a deterioration in water quality occurs. Pools that are less frequently used should be checked before use and then monthly throughout their operational period.

### Hazards associated with disinfectants

Whichever method of disinfection is being used, it is essential that current operating instructions and current safety advice are available from the suppliers. The pool operator, or other person competent to read, understand and interpret the instructions and advice has to produce written safe work procedures, which should usually include:

- safe methods of use/operation of systems;
- goods inwards procedures;
- controls on smoking, eating and drinking;
- storage arrangements;
- emergency alarms and procedures;
- spillage and waste disposal methods;
- first aid.

The hazards associated with these materials are largely those of chemical handling generally. There is also a risk of chlorine gas being generated if chlorine-containing chemicals come into contact with acids, or from contact between certain dry chemicals and water. All the chemicals mentioned in paragraphs 361-378 can cause irritation should they come into contact with the skin.

Advice on the safe design and operation of the most commonly-used disinfecting systems is given in *Swimming pool water - treatment and quality standards*.[13] Some important considerations are discussed in paragraphs 358-387.

### Safety when choosing a disinfectant

**358** Two principles can usefully be applied to start the process of choosing a disinfectant: compatibility with source water, and risk. The two are connected. The better suited the disinfectant is to the source water, the more efficient will be the disinfecting, and consequently the use of chemicals of any kind will be minimised. For example, as a rough rule of thumb, acid waters (often soft waters) suggest an alkaline disinfectant (sodium or calcium hypochlorite); alkaline waters (often hard) with acidic chlorine gas. In general, risks will vary with the properties of the chemical and the way it is used.

**359** There are many ways to disinfect a pool, and the choice can seem complicated. The key considerations are:

- the efficacy of disinfection;
- compatibility with the source water supply (for fill and make-up);
- type and size of pool;
- bathing load, etc;
- operation of the pool;
- training and competency of staff.

**360** However, the issue of safety must be dealt with as the main priority and throughout the water treatment process.

### Chemicals used

#### Calcium hypochlorite

**361** Calcium hypochlorite is a dry and relatively stable compound of chlorine, calcium and oxygen. It must be kept dry and free from contact with all organic materials including paper products, oil and oil products, detergents, cleaning fluids and acids. Contact with organic materials, including isocyanurates and other chemicals, causes a heat reaction, and can lead to explosion, fire and the emission of toxic fumes. Contact with acids liberates toxic chlorine gas.

**362** Spillage should be avoided, as mixture with other chemicals already on the floor or other surfaces could also cause these problems. It should be stored in sealed containers, off wet floors and away from pipes and hot water heaters. There must be 'no smoking' signs in the storage area where this chemical is kept. Suitable personal protection should be used when handling and the provision of an emergency shower considered in large installations.

#### Sodium hypochlorite

**363** Sodium hypochlorite is a liquid; if a liquid acid is used with it, there should be safeguards to prevent any confusion between them. The inadvertent direct mixing of an acid with sodium hypochlorite will liberate toxic chlorine gas and the system should be designed to prevent this taking place.

**364** Carbon dioxide (or carbonic acid) may be used as the acid in some pools. The system works by metering carbon dioxide gas into the water recirculation system. It works best where the total alkalinity of the water supply is less than 150 mg/L of

CaCO₃ and where there are no water features such as wave machines or fountains which expel the carbon dioxide from the water. It has the advantage that, unlike other liquid acid systems, there is no possibility of the accidental generation of chlorine gas.

**365** Storage of liquid carbon dioxide (particularly in a relatively confined space) does, however, carry its own risk: displacement of oxygen, leading to asphyxiation; and toxicity at high concentrations. Cylinders of carbon dioxide should be stored outside buildings in well-ventilated areas. HSE has produced guidance on cylinder storage, bulk storage and the use of liquid carbon dioxide (see Further reading section for detailed guidance).

**366** Sodium hypochlorite can also react vigorously with oxidising materials such as chlorinated isocyanurates.

**367** Suitable personal protective equipment should be used when handling and there should be ready access to an emergency shower where bulk tanks are used.

*Chlorinated isocyanurates*

**368** There is a range of products in this category, with many brand names. They are white or off-white granules or tablets with a chlorine odour. Confusion with other white chemicals must be guarded against. The granules are stable when dry but will slowly liberate chlorine when in contact with water. They can explode in contact with calcium hypochlorite, ammonium salts and other nitrogenous materials and will react vigorously with strong acids, alkalis and reducing agents. Chlorinated isocyanurates should be kept well-sealed in a cool, well-ventilated place, away from combustible materials. Feeders must be designed for the particular chemical, and not used for any other.

*Bromochlorodimethylhydantion*

**369** This product, in stick or tablet form, is stable when dry but will emit bromine/chlorine gas in contact with water. When applied, it is important not to mix the product with other chemicals and to keep it well away from all alkaline substances, eg sodium carbonate, calcium hypochlorite, etc. A circulation feeder device is normally used for the application of this chemical, and it is important that no other chemicals are placed in this device and that, when refilling, splashing should be avoided by lowering the water level. Strong concentrations of this chemical can cause severe burns to the skin and eyes. Bromochlorodimethylhydantion should be stored in safe containers in secure premises which are cool, dry and away from oxidisable materials such as paper, solvents, wood, oil, etc.

*Electrolytic generation of sodium hypochlorite*

**370** This system generates sodium hypochlorite from a brine solution by electrolysis. Paragraphs 371-372 deal with some of the hazards which are associated with this form of disinfection. They are not exhaustive and proper consultation with manufacturers of the system and a properly formulated COSHH assessment will be necessary. Hazards stem mainly from the production of flammable, explosive hydrogen gas.

**371** Hydrogen gas released during the electrolytic process should be vented safely into the open air. Selection and siting of any electrical equipment associated with the electrolytic generator requires careful consideration (see paragraphs 294-313 for further details).

**372** Maintenance of electrical equipment is likely to be a job for specialist staff, but staff should be aware of the general hazards of using electrical equipment near these processes.

### Elemental liquid bromine

**373** This is little used in this country. Elemental liquid bromine requires careful handling. The main risks are of spillage of either liquid bromine itself, or of bromine water. This form of bromine can cause very serious burns in contact with the skin and will produce toxic bromine gas in contact with alkaline materials. Containers should be used and stored within a bunded area, and should be handled gently, to avoid damage.

**374** Adequate supplies of neutralising materials, such as sodium carbonate or sodium thiosulphate solutions, should be available near to hand, and there should be ready access to emergency shower facilities.

### Chlorine gas

**375** We recommend against the use of chlorine gas; however, if you do choose to use it or are already using chlorine gas then there are two methods of applying chlorine gas. Both methods require a specially designed storage area for the chlorine cylinders. In the first method, the chlorine cylinders are stored in a room that is ventilated to fresh air; in the second method, the chlorine is stored in a completely sealed room. Whichever method is used, the installation must comply with *HSE's General COSHH ACOP, Carcinogens ACOP and Biological agents ACOP*[27] and be approved by the local HSE office and the supplier of the gas.

**376** The potential for a serious toxic gas discharge is considerable where chlorine is used in its gaseous form. It is vital to ensure that the building and ancillary areas have been designed to incorporate the requirements for the safe use of chlorine.

**377** It is important that:

- particular care is taken when changing cylinders;
- associated pipework is made of suitable material, adequately supported, and clearly labelled;
- chlorine gas cylinders should be stored only in a purpose-designed room which does not communicate with other parts of the building and which must be made secure. The room must have an exhaust system capable of dealing with minor leaks. In case of a major leak, the exhaust fan should be controllable so that the gas can be dispersed safely under controlled conditions. Minor or major leaks of chlorine gas should disperse safely without any risk to people, so storerooms should not be adjacent to public areas or close to ventilation air intakes where contamination may occur.

**378** Where these conditions cannot be provided then the preferred system is of a totally sealed store where any gas leakage is contained. Any minor gas leakage is removed by scrubbing through a carbon filter or in the case of a major leak is dissolved by the automatic release of a fine water spray. However, pool operators should:

- have a chlorine gas detection system installed in the store. Alarm facilities should be provided, both inside and outside the store, to warn of a chlorine leak;
- ensure employees are adequately trained in the handling and use of chlorine in cylinders;
- ensure suitable personal protective equipment (including respiratory protection) is provided;
- have a written emergency procedure, the contents of which employees are aware.

## Danger of contamination

**379** All chemicals generating chlorine on contact with water (calcium and chlorinated isocyanurate and bromochlorodimethylhydantion) need to be kept cool (temperatures should not exceed 30 °C), in closed containers and away from dampness and contamination by organic materials such as grease. Ammonia is particularly dangerous in contact with chlorinating agents. Some chemicals react with strong acids and some with alkalis or even each other. Do not attempt to mix chemicals, even apparently similar types. Only use chemicals in the specific circulation feeder designed for them.

## Ozone

**380** Guidance on the design, installation, operation and maintenance of ozone systems is given in a British Water Code of Practice 99. Hazards can arise from the other chemicals used (hypochlorite, acid) and from the electrical ozone generating process.

**381** Additional guidance on health hazards associated with ozone has been published by HSE. It is strongly recommended that ozonators are automatically shut down in any of the following abnormal operating conditions:

- air drier failure;
- cooling water failure;
- loss of vacuum (or excess pressure, depending on the system);
- circulation pump failure;
- excess or low electrical power;
- air flow failure.

**382** It is also recommended that the monitoring of ozone in the plant room atmosphere ensures automatic ozonator shutdown at 0.3 mg/L ozone or less, while activating warning alarms at 0.1 mg/L or less. The short-term occupational exposure standard is 0.2 mg/L in any 15-minute period.

**383** Ozone is highly toxic and must not be allowed to go from the treatment plant into the pool. To help prevent this happening there are a number of ways in which ozone levels can be monitored in pool water to indicate if ozone is breaking through the deozonising filter bed and entering the pool.

It is very important that a trained plant engineer is appointed to operate the ozone plant. Ozone equipment should be inspected twice a year and serviced annually.

**General considerations**

In general, the most effective dosing systems are also the safest for bathers and operators:

- Automatic dosing (the type which alters the disinfectant or pH levels to the required levels in response to continual monitoring) is preferred; manual testing of the pool water is required to verify the operation of the automatic system.
- Any system, whether manual or automatic, needs to be maintained. The operation, maintenance and modification of such systems needs to be carried out by competent staff with appropriate training and experience. Systems to ensure this need to be devised and managed.
- The pool water treatment system, including circulation through the filters and dosing equipment, should operate 24 hours a day; however, the dosing equipment should be designed to shut off if the circulation system fails.
- Disinfectants should be dosed *before* the filters, and pH-adjusting chemicals *after* the filters.
- Hand dosing is not recommended. It is rarely justified and only after all relevant health and safety issues have been settled. No chemicals should be added to the pool while bathers are using it, nor should bathers be readmitted until all materials have been fully dissolved and dispersed.
- When descaling dosing lines with acid, the safest possible alternative should always be used (ie sodium bisulphate).
- In all pools, and particularly pools used on an intermittent basis, the disinfectant levels and pH value of the pool water will need to be checked prior to use to ensure the pool is safe.
- Never mix chemicals.

**Monitoring of chemicals in the pool water**

Most disinfectants can be harmful to bathers if incorrectly used. It is therefore important to check on a frequent basis the chemical levels in the pool.

Manual checking of the water by taking appropriate tests for disinfectant and pH levels, together with other chemical tests that are recommended by PWTAG, are a fundamental requirement for all pools. Some pools are fitted with automatic controllers that measure the amounts of disinfectant or the pH of the pool and then vary the dose rate in accordance with the readings. In a pool where these devices are working well and can be relied upon for their accuracy then manually testing the water before the pool is used, after the cessation of use, and one intermediate test, may provide sufficient monitoring. In a pool where dosing is controlled manually, the pool should be tested prior to use and every 2 hours thereafter through to closing.

**Filtration**

Sand filters are commonly used in pool water filters. When filters become dirty they require cleaning by reversing the flow of water through them to drain; this is termed backwashing. Correct backwashing will require the appropriate rate of water through the bed to achieve fluidisation of the sand bed to enable the removal of the dirt and other materials caught in the filter medium. Filters should be cleaned by backwashing at least once a week or more frequently as determined by the difference in pressure between the inlet and outlet. Follow the manufacturer's instructions.

**389** Backwashing can significantly lower the level of the water. It is always safer if backwashing is done when the pool is not in use. If backwashing is undertaken while the pool is in use, a system for maintaining the normal water level should be in operation.

**390** In multiple-filter installations, backwashing should be staggered. This makes it easier to control the pool water level, and reduces the risk that the disinfectant residual will fall below the recommended minimum concentration when the pool water level is restored by the addition of fresh water. Automatic make-up and levelling devices can help maintain the correct water level, especially when backwashing is carried out frequently.

**391** Cleaning or maintenance activities may require employees to enter enclosed spaces such as filter vessels. This should only be done after a comprehensive assessment of the dangers associated with this work, and advice such as that published by HSE and the vessels' manufacturer should be carefully followed. In particular:

- there should be safe entry and exit. Access ports should be large enough to allow easy rescue and there should always be a second person in constant attendance outside. Adequate communication should be maintained between the person in the confined space and the attendant and between the attendant and others with whom they may wish to raise the alarm and institute rescue procedures;
- spaces should be thoroughly ventilated before entry and tested for oxygen deficiency or hazardous gases. Where there is sludge to be removed, the work itself may generate fumes and the person entering should in these circumstances wear suitable breathing apparatus as indicated by the assessment;
- if flammable vapours are present there will be an increased risk in certain circumstances and consideration must be given to sources of ignition including electrical equipment.

**392** People working on or with the sand should bear in mind that it may be contaminated by potentially pathogenic micro-organisms, therefore appropriate personal protective equipment should be worn and close attention paid to personal hygiene.

**Emergency procedures**

*First aid*

**393** The first-aid provisions should include equipment for dealing with the consequences of direct contact with chemicals; for example, by providing eyewash bottles in case of chemicals coming onto contact with the eyes. Eyewash facilities should be located in close proximity to the hazard to enable immediate action. A wash-basin with running water should be provided in case of chemicals coming into contact with the skin. Similarly, it will be appropriate, in circumstances where a member of staff could be subject to severe exposure to a harmful chemical, that full-body douche-type showers are provided for emergency use.

*Chemical spillage*

Any spillage should be cleared away using a safe method. The method for clearing spillage recommended by the supplier and the pool operator should be displayed on a notice together with the provision of the necessary equipment and its location. Care should be taken to prevent any chemical from entering a drain unless it is safe to do so.

*Major leak of toxic gases*

There should be an EAP for dealing with any major release of toxic gas. The procedure should include arrangements for:

- evacuating the whole site, if necessary;
- co-ordinating with the emergency services, including informing them immediately of hazardous substances present (unless they already have this information).

In certain exceptional circumstances (eg where more than 10 t of chlorine are stored) the premises may be subject to the *Notification of Installations Handling Hazardous Substances Regulations 1982*,[28] or the *Control of Major Accident Hazards Regulations 1999*.[29] The local HSE office should be consulted, as necessary.

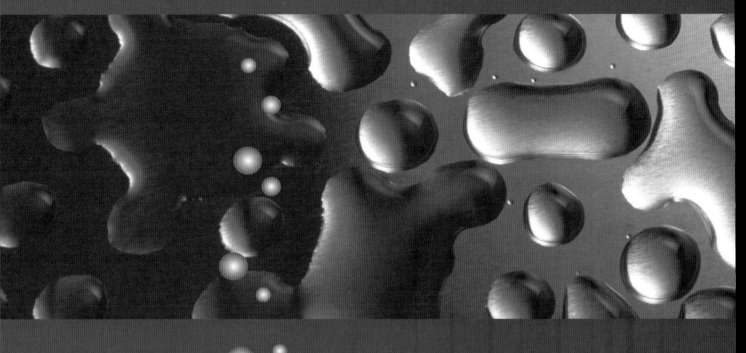

# Appendices

Appendix 1    Membership of independent Working
              Group chaired by HSE

Appendix 2    Safety signs

Appendix 3    Swimming pool user's safety code

Appendix 4    Pool safety operating procedures (PSOP)

Appendix 5    Hire of pool to outside organisations:
              check-list of points for inclusion
              in contracts

Appendix 6    Scottish National Vocational
              Qualifications (S/NVQs)

Appendix 7    Addresses of relevant organisations

Appendix 8    Dimensions for diving equipment

Appendix 9    List of HSE Offices, Sport England
              Offices and Sports Council Offices

Appendix 10   References and further reading

**Appendix 1     Membership of independent Working Group chaired by HSE**

*Acknowledgements*

We gratefully acknowledge the help of the Working Group and all those who contributed to the revision of this safety guidance.  Group members are:

Mr R Riley
Institute of Sport and Recreation Management

Mr J N Winter
Advisor to the English Sports Council

Mr K H Sach
Advisor to the English Sports Council

Mr P A Dawes
Local Authority Environmental Health Officer

Mr S Lear and Mr B Sims
Royal Life Saving Society UK

Ms R Alleyne, Mr D Butler, Ms J Borrow and Mr S Tilbury.
English Sports Council

Representatives from HSE included:
Mr J Russell - Safety Policy Directorate (Chairman)
Mr R McTaggart - Safety Policy Directorate
Ms P Anderson - Safety Policy Directorate
Dr T Williams - Field Operations Directorate

**Appendix 2    Safety signs**

*The requirements of the Health and Safety (Safety Signs and Signals) Regulations 1996*

These Regulations include a description of sign boards which give a health and safety message by use of a combination of geometric shapes, colours and pictograms. The signs must meet the minimum requirement set out in Schedule 1 of the Regulations.

*Examples of signs based upon the Health and Safety (Safety Signs and Signals) Regulations 1996*

The following examples show how the principles of the Health and Safety (Safety Signs and Signals) Regulations 1996 may be applied to safety in swimming pools. The same principles may be applied to other swimming pool activities not covered here.

A guide to the requirements of the Regulations is obtainable from HSE Books.

## Prohibition signs

**No smoking**

**No access for unauthorised persons**

## Warning signs

**Toxic material**          **Corrosive material**          **General danger**

## Information signs

**Fire exit**                          **First-aid post**

**Appendix 3    Swimming pool user's safety code**

*1    Spot the dangers*

Take care, swimming pools can be hazardous.  Water presents a risk of drowning, and injuries can occur from hitting the hard surrounds, or from misuse of the equipment.

Every pool is different, so always make sure you know how deep the water is, and check for other hazards such as diving boards, wave machines, water slides and steep slopes into deeper water, etc.

*2    Always swim within your ability*

Never swim after a heavy meal or after alcohol.  Avoid holding your breath and swimming long distances under water.  Be especially careful if you have a medical condition such as epilepsy, asthma, diabetes or heart problems.

Follow advice provided for the safety of yourself and others.  Avoid unruly behaviour which can be dangerous: for instance, running on the side of the pool, ducking, acrobatics in the water, or shouting or screaming (which could distract attention from an emergency).  Always do as the lifeguards say, and remember that a moment of foolish behaviour can cost a life.

*3    Look out for yourself and other swimmers*

It is safer to swim with a companion.  Keep an eye open for others, particularly younger children and non-swimmers.

*4    Learn how to help*

If you see somebody in difficulty, call for help immediately.  In an emergency, keep calm and do exactly as you are told.

## Appendix 4    Pool safety operating procedures (PSOP)

*Normal Operating Plan (NOP)*

(a) **Details of the pool(s)** - dimensions and depths, features and equipment and a plan of the building.  The plan of the building may include positions of pool alarms, fire alarms, emergency exit routes and any other relevant information.

(b) **Potential risk** - an appreciation of the main hazards and of users particularly at risk is required before safe operating procedures can be identified.

(c) **Dealing with the public** - arrangements for communicating safety messages to customers, customer care, poolside rules for the public and for lifeguards, controlling access.

(d) **Lifeguards' duties and responsibilities** and special supervision requirements for equipment, etc; lifeguard training; and numbers of lifeguards for particular activities.

(e) **Systems of work** including lines of supervision, call-out procedures, work rotation and maximum poolside working times.

(f) **Operational systems**  - controlling access to a pool or pools intended to be out of use including the safe use of pool covers.

(g) **Detailed work instructions** including pool cleaning procedures, safe setting up and checking of equipment, diving procedures and setting up the pool for galas.

(h) **First-aid supplies and training,** including equipment required, its location, arrangements for checking it, first aiders, first-aid training and disposal of sharps.

(i) **Details of alarm systems and any emergency equipment, maintenance arrangements**  - all alarm systems and emergency equipment provided, including operation, location, action to be taken on hearing the alarm, testing arrangements and maintenance.

(j) **Conditions of hire to outside organisations.**

*Emergency Action Plan (EAP)*

Action to be taken in the event of a foreseeable emergency, for example:

(a) overcrowding;
(b) disorderly behaviour (including violence to staff);
(c) lack of water clarity;
(d) outbreak of fire (or sounding of the alarm to evacuate the building);
(e) bomb threat;
(f) lighting failure;
(g) structural failure;
(h) emission of toxic gases;
(i) serious injury to a bather;
(j) discovery of a casualty in the water.

The procedure should make it clear, if it becomes necessary, how to clear the water or evacuate the building.  To ensure the effectiveness of emergency procedures management should ensure:

(a) all staff are adequately trained in such procedures;
(b) notices are displayed to advise the general public of the arrangements;
(c) exit doors, signs, fire-fighting equipment and break-glass call points where provided, should be checked regularly to ensure they are kept free from obstruction;
(d) all fire exit doors are operable without the aid of a key at all times the premises are occupied.

**Appendix 5**   **Hire of pool to outside organisations: check-list of points for inclusion in contracts**

(a)   Information on numbers participating and their swimming skills.

(b)   Name of hirer's representative(s) who will be in charge of the group.

(c)   Numbers and skills/qualifications of lifeguards to be present during the session; and whether these will be provided by the hirer or by the pool operator.

(d)   Hirer to be given copies of normal and emergency operating procedures, and to sign to the effect that these have been read and understood.

(e)   Specific agreement on the respective responsibilities of the pool operator and the hirer for action in any emergency.  A distinction needs to be drawn between:

   i)      emergencies arising from the activities of the group using the pool;
   ii)     other emergencies (structural or power failures, etc).

Responsibility for the latter will remain with the pool operator who will therefore need to have competent staff in attendance during the hire session.

(f)   Any rules of behaviour to be enforced during the session.

(g)   Any advice on safety to be given to participants, eg on avoiding alcohol and food immediately before swimming.

**Appendix 6      Scottish/National Vocational Qualifications (S/NVQs)**

1      Once a lifeguard qualification has been attained then an individual can use the ongoing training programme as a means of progressing towards a Scottish/National Vocational Qualification (S/NVQ). S/NVQs are based on national standards. They provide an assessment of individual competence and test the ability to perform a function in a real work situation to an agreed standard consistently over a period of time. They are assessed independently of any prescribed training route. They do not replace the requirement for training but provide an objective assessment of its effectiveness.

2      S/NVQ units relating to the duties of a lifeguard are to:
   ■      maintain the safety of swimming pool users;
   ■      deal with accidents and emergencies;
   ■      develop and maintain positive work relationships with customers;
   ■      make information and advice available to customers;
   ■      contribute to maintaining a safe and secure environment.

3      Further information on how to gain S/NVQs can be obtained from the National Training Organisation for Sport and Recreation and Allied Occupations (see Appendix 7 for addresses).

The National Training Organisation for
Sport and Recreation and Allied
Occupations
24 Stephenson Way
London NW1 2HD
Tel:  0171 388 7755
Fax: 0171 388 9733

**Organisations who can advise on training
or general safety matters**

*Organisations providing first-aid training*

St John Ambulance
1 Grosvenor Crescent
London SW1X 7EF
Tel:  0171 235 5231
Fax: 0171 235 0796

St Andrew Ambulance Association
St Andrew's House
48 Milton Street
Glasgow G4 OHR
Tel:  0141 332 4031
Fax: 0141 332 6582

British Red Cross Society
9 Grosvenor Crescent
London SW1X 7EJ
Tel:  0171 235 5454
Fax: 0171 245 6315

*Organisations providing pool attendants'
and plant operators' training*

The Institute of Leisure and Amenity
Management
ILAM House
Lower Basildon
Reading
Berkshire RG8 9NE
Tel: 01491 874800
Fax: 01491 874801

Institute of Sport and Recreation
Management
Giffard House
36-38 Sherrard Street
Melton Mowbray
Leicestershire LE13 1XJ
Tel: 01664 565531
Fax: 01664 501155

*Organisations providing lifeguard,
lifesaving or swimming training*

The Royal Life Saving Society UK
River House
High Street
Broom
Warwickshire B50 4HN
Tel:  01789 773994
Fax: 01789 773995

Amateur Swimming Association
Harold Fern House
Derby Square
Loughborough
LE11 5AL
Tel:  01509 618700
Fax: 01509 618701

Scottish Amateur Swimming Association
Holmhills Farm
Greenlees Road
Cambuslang
Glasgow G72 8DT
Tel:  0141 641 8818
Fax: 0141 641 4443

Welsh Amateur Swimming Association
Roth Park House
Ninian Road
Cardiff CF2 5ER
Tel:  01222 488820
Fax: 01222 488820

The Swimming Teachers' Association
Anchor House
Birch Street
Walsall
West Midlands WS2 8HZ
Tel:  01922 645097
Fax: 01922 720628

*Organisations who can advise on child
protection*

The NSPCC
National Centre
42 Curtain Road
London EC2A 3NH
Tel:  0171 825 2500
Helpline:  0800 800500

The National Coaching Foundation
114 Cardigan Road
Headingley
Leeds LS6 3BJ
Tel: 0113 274 4802
Fax: 0113 275 5019

*Organisations who can advise on supervision of specialised activities*

British Canoe Union
John Dudderidge House
Adbolton Lane
West Bridgford
Nottingham NG2 5AS
Tel: 0115 982 1100
Fax: 0115 982 1797

The British Sub-Aqua Club
Telford's Quay
Ellesmere Port
South Wirral
Cheshire L65 4FY
Tel: 0151 350 6200
Fax: 0151 350 6215

Scottish Canoe Association
Caledonia House
South Gyle
Edinburgh EH12 9DQ
Tel: 0131 317 7314
Fax: 0131 317 7319

Scottish Sub-Aqua Club
Cockburn Centre
40 Bogmoor Place
Glasgow G51 4TQ
Tel: 0141 425 1021
Fax: 0141 425 1021

*Safety organisations*

Royal Society for the Prevention of Accidents (RoSPA)
Edgbaston Park
353 Bristol Road
Birmingham B5 7ST
Tel: 0121 248 2000
Fax: 0121 248 2001

Scottish Accident Prevention Council
Water Leisure Safety Committee
Slateford House
53 Lanark Road
Edinburgh EH14 1TL
Tel: 0131 455 7457
Fax: 0131 443 9442

British Safety Council
National Safety Centre
70 Chancellors Road
London W6 9RS
Tel: 0181 741 1231
Fax: 0181 741 4555

*Organisations who can provide advice on disabilities*

British Epilepsy Association
Anstey House
40 Hanover Square
Leeds LS3 1BE
Tel: 0113 243 9393
Fax: 0113 242 8804

National Society for Epilepsy
Chalfont St Peter
Gerrards Cross
Bucks SL9 0RJ
Tel: 01494 601300
Fax: 01494 871927

Epilepsy Association of Scotland
48 Govan Road
Glasgow G51 1JL
Tel: 0141 427 4911
Fax: 0141 427 7414

Epilepsy Wales
15 Chester Street
St Asaph
Denbighshire
LL17 0RE
Tel: 01341 423339
Fax: 01341 423993

Disability Sport England
13 Brunswick Place
London
N1 6DX
Tel: 0171 490 4919
Fax: 0171 490 4914

UKSAPLD (UK Sports Association for
People with Learning Disability)
Ground Floor
Leroy House
436 Essex Road
London N1 3QP
Tel:  0171 354 1030
Fax: 0171 354 2593

English Sports Association for People with
Learning Disabilities
Unit 9
Milner Way
Ossett
West Yorkshire WF5 9JN
Tel:  01924 267 555

British Paralympic Association
Room 514, Impact House
2 Edbridge Road
Croydon
Surrey CR9 1PJ
Tel:  0181 681 9655

National Asthma Campaign
Providence House
Providence Place
London N1 0NT
Tel:  0345 010203

Royal National Institute for the Blind
224 Great Portland Street
London W1N 6AA
Tel:  0171 388 1266
Fax: 0171 388 2034

Royal National Institute for the Deaf
19-23 Featherstone Street
London EC1Y 8SL
Tel:  0171 296 8134
Fax: 0171 296 8070

Scottish Disability Sport
Fife Institute of Physical and Recreational
Education
Viewfield Road
Glenrothes
Fife KY6 2RB
Tel:  01592 415 700
Fax: 01592 415 710

Disability Scotland
Princes House
5 Shandwick Place
Edinburgh EH2 4RG
Tel:  0131 229 8632
Fax: 0131 229 5168

Deaf Broadcasting Council
70 Blacketts Wood Drive
Chorleywood
Herts
Tel:  01923 283127
Fax: 01923 283127

Deaf Society
Abbey Hall
Rock Road
Torquay
Devon
Tel:  01803 607144

British Deaf Association
1-3 Worship Street
London EC2A 2AB
Tel:  0171 588 3520
Fax: 0171 588 3527

*Organisations that can offer advice on
buildings and non-slip floors*

The Building Research Establishment
Bucknalls Lane
Garston
Watford WD2 7JR
Tel:  01923 664664

The Institute of Swimming Pool Engineers
(ISPE)
PO Box 3098,
Halstead
Essex CO9 4SB
Tel:  01440 785999

National Master Tile Fixers Association
Forum Court
83 Copers Cope Road
Beckenham
Kent BR3 1NR

# Appendix 8    Dimensions for diving equipment

**FINA Dimensions for Diving facilities** — as of 3 March 1991 (see FR5.3.1)

| | | Springboard 1 Metre HORI | Springboard 1 Metre VERT | Springboard 3 Metres HORI | Springboard 3 Metres VERT | Platform 1 Metre HORI | Platform 1 Metre VERT | Platform 3 Metres HORI | Platform 3 Metres VERT | Platform 5 Metres HORI | Platform 5 Metres VERT | Platform 7.5 Metres HORI | Platform 7.5 Metres VERT | Platform 10 Metres HORI | Platform 10 Metres VERT |
| --- | --- | --- | --- | --- | --- | --- | --- | --- | --- | --- | --- | --- | --- | --- | --- |
| | LENGTH | 4.80 | | 4.80 | | 5.00 | | 5.00 | | 6.00 | | 6.00 | | 6.00 | |
| | WIDTH | 0.50 | | 0.50 | | 0.60 | | 0.60 min 1.5pref. | | 1.50 | | 1.50 | | 2.00 | |
| | HEIGHT | 1.00 | | 3.00 | | 0.60–1.00 | | 2.60–3.00 | | 5.00 | | 7.50 | | 10.00 | |
| **A** From plummet BACK TO POOL WALL | Designation | A-1 | | A-3 | | A-1pl | | A-3pl | | A-5 | | A-7.5 | | A-10 | |
| | Minimum | 1.50 | | 1.50 | | 0.75 | | 1.25 | | 1.25 | | 1.50 | | 1.50 | |
| | Preferred | 1.80 | | 1.80 | | 0.75 | | 1.25 | | 1.25 | | 1.50 | | 1.50 | |
| **A/A** From plummet BACK TO PLATFORM plummet directly below | Designation | | | | | | | | | A/A5/1 | | A/A5/3.1 | | a/A10/5.3.1 | |
| | Minimum | | | | | | | | | 0.75 | | 0.75 | | 0.75 | |
| | Preferred | | | | | | | | | 1.25 | | 1.25 | | 1.25 | |
| **B** From plummet to POOL WALL AT SIDE | Designation | B-1 | | B3 | | B-1pl | | B-3pl | | B-5 | | B-7.5 | | B-10 | |
| | Minimum | 2.50 | | 3.50 | | 2.30 | | 2.80 | | 3.25 | | 4.25 | | 5.25 | |
| | Preferred | 2.50 | | 3.50 | | 2.30 | | 2.90 | | 3.75 | | 4.50 | | 5.25 | |
| **C** From plummet to ADJACENT PLUMMET | Designation | C1-1 | | C3-3,3-1 | | C1-1pl | | C3-3PL,1pl | | C5-3,5-1 | | C7.5-5,3.1 | | C10-7.5,5,3.1 | |
| | Minimum | 2.00 | | 2.20 | | 1.65 | | 2.00 | | 2.25 | | 2.50 | | 2.75 | |
| | Preferred | 2.40 | | 2.60 | | 1.95 | | 2.10 | | 2.50 | | 2.50 | | 2.75 | |
| **D** From plummet to POOL WALL AHEAD | Designation | D-1 | | D-3 | | D-1pl | | D-3pl | | D-5 | | D-7.5 | | D-10 | |
| | Minimum | 9.00 | | 10.25 | | 8.00 | | 9.50 | | 10.25 | | 11.00 | | 13.50 | |
| | Preferred | 9.00 | | 10.25 | | 8.00 | | 9.50 | | 10.25 | | 11.00 | | 13.50 | |
| **E** From plummet on BOARD TO CEILING | Designation | | E-1 | | E-3 | | E-1pl | | E-3pl | | E-5 | | E-7.5 | | E-10 |
| | Minimum | | 5.00 | | 5.00 | | 3.25 | | 3.25 | | 3.25 | | 3.25 | | 4.00 |
| | Preferred | | 5.00 | | 5.00 | | 3.50 | | 3.50 | | 3.50 | | 3.50 | | 5.00 |
| **F** CLEAR OVERHEAD behind and each side of plummet | Designation | F-1 | | F-3 | | F-1pl | | F-3pl | | F-5 | | F-7.5 | | F-10 | |
| | Minimum | 2.50 | | 2.50 | | 2.75 | | 2.75 | | 2.75 | | 2.75 | | 2.75 | |
| | Preferred | 2.50 | | 2.50 | | 2.75 | | 2.75 | | 2.75 | | 2.75 | | 2.75 | |
| **G** CLEAR OVERHEAD ahead of plummet | Designation | G-1 | | G-3 | | G-1pl | | G-3pl | | G-5 | | G-7.5 | | G-10 | |
| | Minimum | 5.00 | | 5.00 | | 5.00 | | 5.00 | | 5.00 | | 5.00 | | 6.00 | |
| | Preferred | 5.00 | | 5.00 | | 5.00 | | 5.00 | | 5.00 | | 5.00 | | 6.00 | |
| **H** DEPTH OF WATER at plummet | Designation | | H-1 | | H-3 | | H-1pl | | H-3pl | | H-5 | | H-7.5 | | H-10 |
| | Minimum | | 3.40 | | 3.70 | | 3.20 | | 3.50 | | 3.70 | | 4.10 | | 4.50 |
| | Preferred | | 3.50 | | 3.80 | | 3.30 | | 3.60 | | 3.80 | | 4.50 | | 5.00 |
| **J K** DISTANCE AND DEPTH ahead of plummet | Designation | J-1 | K-1 | J-3 | K-3 | J-1pl | K-1pl | J-3pl | K-3pl | J-5 | K-5 | J-7.5 | K-7.5 | J-10 | K-10 |
| | Minimum | 5.00 | 3.30 | 6.00 | 3.60 | 4.50 | 3.10 | 5.50 | 3.40 | 6.00 | 3.60 | 8.00 | 4.00 | 11.00 | 4.25 |
| | Preferred | 5.00 | 3.40 | 6.00 | 3.70 | 4.50 | 3.20 | 5.50 | 3.50 | 6.00 | 3.70 | 8.00 | 4.40 | 11.00 | 4.75 |
| **L M** DISTANCE AND DEPTH each side of plummet | Designation | L-1 | M-1 | L-3 | M-3 | L-1pl | M-1pl | L-3pl | M-3pl | L-5 | M-5 | L-7.5 | M-7.5 | L-10 | M-10 |
| | Minimum | 1.50 | 3.30 | 2.00 | 3.60 | 1.40 | 3.10 | 1.80 | 3.40 | 3.00 | 3.60 | 3.75 | 4.00 | 4.50 | 4.25 |
| | Preferred | 2.00 | 3.40 | 2.50 | 3.70 | 1.90 | 3.20 | 2.30 | 3.50 | 3.50 | 3.70 | 4.50 | 4.40 | 5.25 | 4.75 |
| **N** MAXIMUM SLOPE TO REDUCE DIMENSIONS beyond full requirments | POOL DEPTH CEILING HT. | 30 degrees | | 30 degrees | | | | | | | | | | | |

**NOTE:** Dimensions **C** (plummet to adjacent plummet) apply to Platforms with widths as detailed. If platform widths are increased then **C** is to be increased by half the additional width(s).

Reproduced from 1998/2000 FINA handbook. In subsequent years a copy of the current FINA information should be sought from the Amateur Swimming Association (ASA)

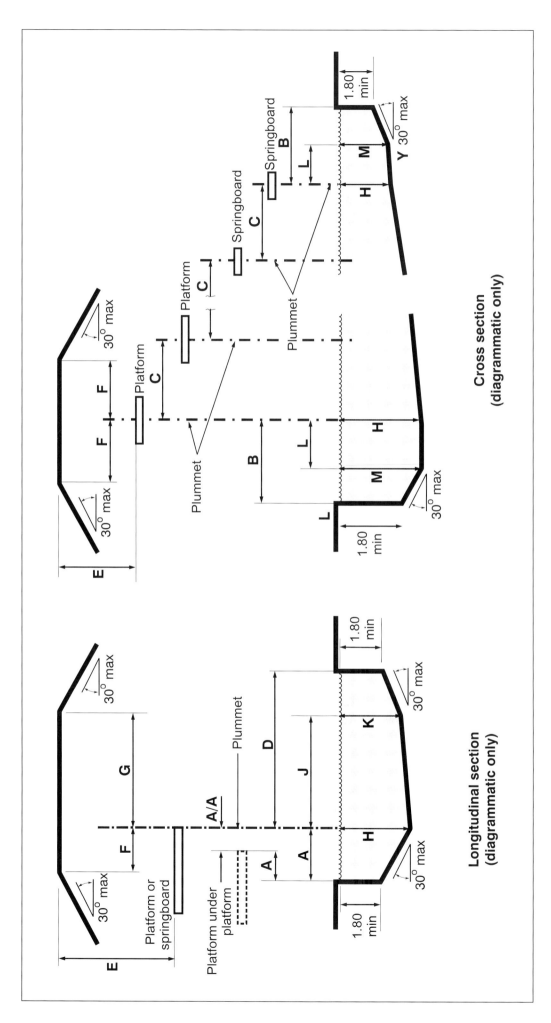

**Longitudinal section (diagrammatic only)**

**Cross section (diagrammatic only)**

## HSE offices

### West Region
Inter City House
Mitchell Lane
Victoria Street
Bristol BS1 6AN
Tel: 0117 988 6000

### Home Counties
Priestley House
Priestley Road
Basingstoke
Hants RG24 9NW
Tel: 01256 404000

### South East
3 East Grinstead House
London Road
East Grinstead
West Sussex RH19 1RR
Tel: 01342 334200

### London South East
St Dunstans House
201-211 Borough High
Street
London SE1 1GZ
Tel: 0171 556 2100

### East Anglia
39 Baddow Road
Chelmsford
Essex CM2 0HL
Tel: 01245 706200

### Northern Home Counties
14 Cardiff Road
Luton
Beds LU1 1PP
Tel: 01582 444200

### East Midlands
5th Floor, Belgrave House
1 Greyfriars
Northampton NN1 2BS
Tel: 01604 738300

### West Midlands
McLaren Building
35 Dale End
Birmingham B4 7NP
Tel: 0121 607 6200

### Wales
Brunel House
2 Fitzalan Road
Cardiff CF2 1SH
Tel: 01222 263000

### Marches
The Marches House
Midway
Newcastle-under-Lyme
Staff ST5 1DT
Tel: 01782 602300

### North Midlands
1st Floor, The Pearson
Building
55 Upper Parliament Street
Nottingham NG1 6AU
Tel: 0115 971 2800

### South Yorkshire and North East Region
Sovereign House
110 Queen Street
Sheffield S1 2ES
Tel: 0114 291 2300

### West and North Yorkshire
8 St Paul's Street
Leeds LS1 2LE
Tel: 0113 283 4200

### Greater Manchester
Quay House
Quay Street
Manchester M3 3JB
Tel: 0161 952 8200

### Merseyside
The Triad
Stanley Road
Bootle L20 3PG
Tel: 0151 479 2200

### North West
Victoria House
Ormskirk Road
Preston PR1 1HH
Tel: 01772 836200

### North East
Arden House
Regent Centre
Gosforth
Newcastle-upon-Tyne
NE3 3JN
Tel: 0191 202 6200

### Scotland West
375 West George Street
Glasgow G2 4LW
Tel: 0141 275 3000

### Scotland East
Belford House
59 Belford Road
Edinburgh EH4 3UE
Tel: 0131 247 2000

## Sport England offices

Sport England
Head office
16 Upper Woburn Place
London WC1H 0QP
Tel: 0171 273 1500
Fax: 0171 383 5740

Sport England Publications
PO Box 255
Wetherby LS23 7LZ
Tel: 0990 210255
Fax: 0990 210266

*Sport England regional offices*

**East**
Crescent House
19 The Crescent
Bedford MK40 2QP
Tel: 01234 345222
Fax: 01234 359046

**East Midlands**
Grove House
Bridgford Road
West Bridgford
Nottingham NG2 6AP
Tel: 0115 982 1887
Fax: 0115 945 5236

**London and South East**
Crystal Palace National
Sports Centre
PO Box 480
London SE19 2BQ
Tel: 0181 778 8600
Fax: 0181 676 9812

**North**
Aykley Heads
Durham DH1 5UU
Tel: 0191 384 9595
Fax: 0191 384 5807

**North West**
Astley House
Quay Street
Manchester M3 4AE
Tel: 0161 834 0338
Fax: 0161 835 3678

**South**
51a Church Street
Caversham
Reading
RG4 8AX
Tel: 0118 948 3311
Fax: 0118 947 5935

**South West**
Ashlands House
Ashlands
Crewkerne
Somerset TA18 7LQ
Tel: 01460 73491
Fax: 01460 77263

**West Midlands**
Metropolitan House
1 Hagley Road
Five Ways
Birmingham B16 8TT
Tel: 0121 456 3444
Fax: 0121 456 1583

**Yorkshire**
Coronet House
Queen Street
Leeds
LS1 4PY
Tel: 0113 243 6443
Fax: 0113 242 2189

**Home Country Sports Councils**

**Sports Council for Wales**
National Sports Centre for
Wales
Sophia Gardens
Cardiff CF1 9SW
Tel: 01222 300500
Fax: 01222 300600

**Sports Council for Northern Ireland**
House of Sport
Upper Malone Road
Belfast BT9 5LA
Tel: 01232 381222
Fax: 01232 682757

**Scottish Sports Council**
Caledonia House
South Gyle
Edinburgh EH12 9DQ
Tel: 0131 317 7200
Fax: 0131 317 7202

## Appendix 10    References and further reading

**References**

Note: Leaflets published by HSE are available from HSE offices (see Appendix 9) and HSE Books. Sport England publications are available from Sport England Publications (address given on page ii).

1       *Pool lifeguard - training manual*
        Royal Life Saving Society (1997) ISBN 0 7234 3057 8

2       *The treatment and quality of swimming pool water* (4th ed) DETR 1984
        ISBN 0 11 751757 7

3       *Recreation management* Facilities Factfile 1 English Sports Council 1994

4       *5 steps to risk assessment* INDG163 (rev) HSE Books 1998

5       *Everyone's guide to RIDDOR '95* HSE31 HSE Books 1996 (Being revised)

6       *Guide to the Reporting of Injuries, Diseases and Dangerous Occurrences Regulations 1995* L73 HSE Books 1996 ISBN 0 7176 1012 8

7       *Wall and floor tiling. Part 3 Code of Practice for the design and installation of ceramic floor tiles and mosaics* BS 5385: Part 3 1989 (amended 1992)

8       *Code of practice for glazing for buildings. Part 4 Safety related to human impact* BS 6262: Part 4 1994

9       *Handbook of sports and recreational building design* (2nd ed) Volume 3 *Ice rinks and swimming pools* Butterworth - Heinemann 1996 ISBN 0 7506 2256 3

10      *Water slides over 2 m in height* BS EN 1069-1: 1996

11      *Safety in machinery* BS 5304: 1988

12      *Requirement for electrical installations, IEE wiring regulations* (16th edn) BS 7671: 1992

13      *Swimming pool water - treatment and quality standards* Pool Water Treatment Advisory Group 1999 ISBN 0 9517007 6 6

14      *Managing asbestos in workplace buildings* INDG223 HSE Books 1996

15      *Storage of LPG at fixed installations* HSG34 HSE Books 1987 ISBN 0 11 883908 X

16      *Workplace health, safety and welfare. The Workplace (Health, Safety and Welfare) Regulations 1992. Approved Code of Practice and guidance* L24 HSE Books 1992 ISBN 0 7176 0413 6

17      *Lighting at work* HSG38 HSE Books 1997 ISBN 0 7176 1232 5

18      *Plugs, socket outlets and couplers for industrial purposes. Part 2 Dimensional interchangeability requirements for pin and contact tube accessories* BS EN 60309: Part 2 1998

19      *Code of practice for the selection, installation and maintenance of electrical apparatus for use in potentially explosive atmospheres (other than mining applications or explosives processing and manufacture)* BS 5345: 1989 (superseded by BS EN 60079-14: 1997)

20      *Electrical apparatus for explosive atmospheres with type of protection N* BS 6941: 1988

21    *Isolating transformers and safety isolating transformers* BS 3535: 1990

22    *Maintaining portable electrical equipment in offices and other low risk environments*
      INDG236 HSE Books 1996

23    *A step-by-step guide to COSHH assessment* HSG97 HSE Books 1992
      ISBN 0 7176 1446 8

24    *Personal eye protection specifications* BS EN 166: 1996

25    *Manual handling. Manual Handling Operations Regulations 1992. Guidance on the
      Regulations* L23 HSE Books 1992 ISBN 0 7176 0411 X

26    *Manual handling - Solutions you can handle*  HSG115 HSE Books 1994
      ISBN 0 7176 0693 7

27    *General COSHH ACOP, Carcinogens ACOP and Biological Agents ACOP. Control of
      Substances Hazardous to Health Regulations 1994. Approved Codes of Practice*  L5
      HSE Books 1997 ISBN 0 7176 1308 9 (revision due spring 1999, ISBN 0 7176 1670 3)

28    *Notification of Installations Handling Hazardous Substances Regulations 1982*
      SI 1982/877

29    *Control of Major Accident Hazards Regulations 1999 (SI No not available at the time of
      going to print)*

**Further reading**

*A Guide to the Health and Safety at Work etc Act 1974* (5th ed)
HSE Books 1992 ISBN 0 7176 044 1

*The Act Outlined* HSC2 HSE Books 1975

*Health and Safety at Work etc Act 1974: Advice to Employers*  HSC3 HSE Books 1975

*Health and Safety at Work etc Act 1974: Advice to Employees* HSC5 HSE Books 1975

*Management of health and safety at work. Management of Health and Safety at Work Regulations
1992. Approved Code of Practice* HSE Books 1992 ISBN 0 7176 0412 8

*A Guide to the Health and Safety (Consultation with Employees) Regulations 1996*
L95 HSE Books 1996 ISBN 0 7176 1234 1

*Consulting Employees on Health and Safety: A guide to the Law*
INDG232 HSE Books 1996

*Workplace health, safety and welfare - A short guide for managers*
INDG170 HSE Books 1995

*Safe use of work equipment* L22 HSE Books 1998 ISBN 0 7176 1626 6

*Managing construction for health and safety. Construction (Design and
Management) Regulations 1994. Approved Code of Practice* L54  HSE Books 1995
ISBN 0 7176 0792 5

*CDM Regulations - How the Regulations affect you* PML54 HSE Books 1995

*Guide to the Construction (Health, Safety and Welfare) Regulations 1996* INDG220
HSE Books 1996

*Electricity at work: Safe working practices* HSG85 HSE Books 1993 ISBN 0 7176 0442 X

*Getting to grips with manual handling: A short guide for employers*
INDG143 HSE Books 1993

*COSHH - The new brief guide for employers* INDG136 HSE Books 1993

*The Diving at Work Regulations 1997* Stationery Office ISBN 0 11 065170 7

*Commercial diving projects inland/inshore. Diving at Work Regulations 1997.*
*Approved Code of Practice* L104 HSE Books 1998 ISBN 0 7176 1495 6

*Recreational diving projects. Diving at Work Regulations 1997.*
*Approved Code of Practice* L105 HSE Books 1998 ISBN 0 7176 1496 4

*Media diving projects. Diving at Work Regulations 1997.*
*Approved Code of Practice* L106 HSE Books 1998 ISBN 0 7176 1497 2

*Scientific and archaeological diving projects. Diving at Work Regulations 1997.*
*Approved Code of Practice* L107 HSE Books 1998 ISBN 0 7176 1497 0

*Are you involved in a diving project?* INDG266 HSE Books 1998

*Writing a safety policy statement: Advice for employers* HSC6 HSE Books 1990

*Managing health and safety - five steps to success* INDG275 HSE Books 1998

*A guide to RIDDOR '95* plus electronic versions of Forms F2508/F2508a on
diskette HSE Books 1996 ISBN 0 7176 1080 2

*First aid at work. Health and Safety (First-Aid) Regulations 1981. Approved Code of*
*Practice and guidance* L74 HSE Books 1997 ISBN 0 7176 1050 0

*First aid training and qualifications for the purposes of the Health and Safety (First-Aid)*
*Regulations 1981* HSE Books 1997 ISBN 0 7176 1347 X

*First aid at work* INDG4 HSE Books 1993 Out of Print

*First aid at work - Your questions answered* INDG214 HSE Books 1997

*Basic advice on first aid at work* INDG215 HSE Books 1997

*Safety signs and signals. The Health and Safety (Safety Signs and Signals) Regulations 1996.*
*Guidance on Regulations* L64 HSE Books 1997 ISBN 0 7176 0870 0

*Signpost to the Health and Safety (Safety Signs and Signals) Regulations 1996* INDG184
HSE Books 1996

*Safety signs and colours. Part 1 Colour and design* BS 5378: Part 1 1980

*Safety signs and colours. Part 2 Colormetric and photometric properties of materials* BS 5378:
Part 2 1980

*Safety signs and colours. Part 3 Specific for additional signs to those given in Part 1* BS 5378:
Part 3 1982

*Fire safety signs, notices and graphic symbols. Part 1 Fire safety notices* BS 5499: Part 1 1990
(amended 1993)

*Fire safety signs, notices and graphic symbols. Part 3 Internally illuminated fire safety signs*
BS 5499: Part 3 1990

*Portable fire extinguishers* BS 5423 1987

*Fire detection and alarm systems for buildings* BS 5839: 1988

*Sound systems for emergency purposes* BS 7443: 1991

*Slips and trips: Guidance for employers on identifying hazards and controlling risks* HSG115 HSE Books 1996 ISBN 0 7176 1145 0

*Preventing slips, trips and falls* INDG225 HSE Books 1996

*The RLSS UK national pool lifeguard qualification (6th edition)* Syllabus and assessment guide available from The Institute of Sport and Recreation Management (ISRM) or The Royal Life Saving Society UK (RLSS) UK 1997

*Safe supervision for teaching and coaching swimming* issued by the Amateur Swimming Association, ISRM, Institute of Swimming Teachers and Coaches RLSS UK 1996

*Specially safe* (Guidance for supervision of people with disabilities) RLSS UK 1995 ISBN  0907082 718

*Guidance on open water sites* RLSS UK and the Royal Society for the Prevention of Accidents (available from Spring 1999)

*Footbaths, showers and pre-swim hygiene* Information sheet 21 ISRM

*Admissions policy for public swimming - Further definition of interpretation* ISRM 1995

*Violence at work: A guide for employers* INDG69 (rev) HSE Books 1996

*Child protection procedures for sport and recreational centres* ISRM 1997 ISBN 1 900 738 40 0

*Protecting children - A guide for sports people*  National Coaching Foundation and the NSPCC 1995 Available from Coachwise Tel: 0113 231 1310

*Our duty of child care Northern Ireland* Child Care NI 1995 Tel: 01232 234499

*Diving in swimming pools and open water* ISRM 1998 ISBN 1 900 738 60 0

*Lifeguards for sub-aqua pool sessions* Information sheet T1 The British Sub-Aqua Club

Stevens T R and Jenkins I *Improving the safety of water slides*  The Safety in Leisure Research Unit 1990 ISBN 0951 5935 01

*Use of play equipment in swimming pools - A suggested code of practice* ISRM 1994 ISBN 0951 5054 40

*Soft play and inflatables* The Institute of Leisure and Amenity Management  1992 ISBN 1 873903 02 2

*Legionnaires' disease* IAC27(rev) HSE Books 1992

*The prevention or control of legionellosis (including Legionnaires' disease)* Approved Code of Practice L8 HSE Books 1995   ISBN 0 7176 0732 1

*The control of legionellosis, including Legionnaires' disease* HSG70 HSE Books 1993 ISBN 0 7176 0451 9

*Safe pressure systems*  INDS27 HSE Books 1996

*Safety of pressure systems. Pressure Systems and Transportable Gas Containers Regulations 1989. Approved Code of Practice* COP37  HSE Books 1990 ISBN 0 11 885514 X

*Guide to the Pressure Systems and Transportable Gas Containers Regulations 1989* HSR30  HSE Books 1990 ISBN 0 7176 0489 6

*Entry into confined spaces* GS5 HSE Books 1994 ISBN 0 7176 0787 9

*Asbestos: The effects on health of exposure to asbestos* (R Doll and J Peto) HSE Books 1996
ISBN 0 7176 1075 6

*Asbestos and you* INDG107 HSE Books 1996 (Being revised)

*Workplace health and safety: Glazing* INDG212 HSE Books 1996

*Windows, doors and rooflights. Part 1 Code of Practice for safety in use and during cleaning of windows and doors* BS 8213: Part 1 1991

*Electrical safety and you* INDG231 HSE Books 1996

*The use of electrical equipment and appliances near a swimming pool* Information sheet number 10 Amateur Swimming Association 1996

*Maintaining portable and transportable electrical equipment* HSG107 HSE Books 1994
ISBN 0 7176 0715 1

*Safety on British beaches - Operational guidelines* 1993 *(1st ed)*
RLSS UK and the Royal Society for the Prevention of Accidents ISBN 0 9070 8295 5

*Programmable electronic systems in safety related applications: An introductory guide* PESOI
HSE Books 1987 ISBN 0 7176 1278 3

*Programmable electronic systems in safety related applications: General technical guidelines*
HSE Books 1987 ISBN 0 11 883906 3

*Stainless steel in swimming pool buildings A guide to selection and use* Nickel Development Institute 1995 Publication number 12010

*The good practice guides* published as part of the *Best practice programme by BRECSU* The Building Research Establishment

*Handbook of sports and recreational building design* (second edition) *Volume 3: Ice rinks and swimming pools* Butterworth-Heinemann 1996 ISBN 0 7506 2256 3

**Sport England guidance notes** (available from Sport England Publications):

*Swimming pools - Design* Sport England 1999 ISBN 1 86078 099 7

*Swimming pools - Improvements and alterations to existing pools* English Sports Council 1994 ISBN 1 872158 98 6

*Swimming pools - Building services* English Sports Council 1995 ISBN 1 872158 99 4

*Access for disabled people* English Sports Council 1998 ISBN 1 872158 54 4

**Scottish Sports Council technical digests** (available from Scottish Sports Council Publications):

*Building in ability: Provision for people with disabilities* Scottish Sports Council 1995
ISBN 1 850603 00 6

*Swimming pools: Changing accommodation* Scottish Sports Council 1995
ISBN 1 850603 45 6

*Swimming pools: Improvements and alterations* Scottish Sports Council 1995
ISBN 1 850603 40 5

*Swimming pools: Small pool design* Scottish Sports Council 1995 ISBN 1 850603 35 9

*Swimming pools: Building services* Scottish Sports Council 1995 ISBN 1 850603 50 2

# INDEX

access
    controlling 38, 65, 67–69, 80
    unauthorised 56, 67–68
access *see also* steps and ladders
accidents and incidents 14–15, 33, 56, 67
acoustic signals *see* signs and signals
air-conditioning *see* heating, ventilation and air-conditioning
alarm systems 67, 69, 82
alcohol consumption 55, 65, 110
ammonia 101
aqua aerobics 85
ASA standards 49, 117
Asbestos (Licensing) Regulations 1983 81
audio equipment 85
automated extended defibrillation (AED) 58
backwashing 102–103
bacteriological sampling *see* also micro-organisms 97
bathers
    education 56, 110
    numbers 62, 67, 68
    risks v
    supervision 34, 57
British Standard 5304:1988 28
British Standard 5345:1989 85
British Standard 5385:Part 3 24
British Standard 6262:Part 4 25
British Standard 6941:1988 85
British Standard 7671:1992 40, 84, 86
British Standard EN 166:1996 92
British Standards EN 1069:Part 1 1996 27
British Water Code of Practice 99 101
bromine 93, 99, 100
bromochloromethylhydantoin 99
bulkheads *see* movable floors and bulkheads
calcium hypochlorite 98
canoeing 72, 115
carbon dioxide (carbonic acid) 98–99
cardiopulmonary resuscitation (CPR) *see* resuscitation
casualties 38, 58, 61
changing areas 64, 70, 80, 81
chemicals
    delivery, storage and handling 93–95, 101
    emergency procedures 103–104
    risk assessment 91, 95
    safe working practices 89–90
    spillages 98, 104
chemicals *see also* hazardous substances
Chemicals (Hazard, Information and Packaging for Supply) Regulations 1994 90
children 56, 65, 68, 69–70, 115
chlorinated isocyanurates 98, 99, 101
chlorine 93, 94, 95, 97, 98, 99, 100, 101
circulation feeders 96–97
circulation of people, design problems 23, 34–38
cleaning and maintenance 80, 83, 103
clubs, pool hire and programmed sessions 14, 65, 71
Confined Spaces Regulations 1997 9, 81
Construction (Design and Management) Regulations 1994 7
Control of Asbestos at Work Regulations 1987 81
Control of Industrial Major Accident Hazards Regulations 1984 104
Control of Substances Hazardous to Health (COSHH) Regulations 1994 60, 90–92, 97
dangerous occurrence, definition 15
design
    advisory organisations 116
    circulation feeder system 96
    identifying and managing problems 32–53
    risks to bathers 90
    swimming pools 19–20
    water treatment systems 96
designers and constructors, responsibilities 1
DIN 51097 42
disco swimming 72
disinfection 89–90, 95–98

diving 29, 56, 70–71
Diving at Work Regulations 1997 8–9, 79
diving facilities and pools
    access and supervision 49, 73
    design 25–26, 41, 49–50, 117–118
dosing systems 95–96, 102
drainage gullies 25, 43
electrical installations and equipment
    location 40, 84, 85, 86
    maintenance 85–87, 100
    portable 85
    safety issues 83–85, 86
Electricity at Work Regulations 1989 7, 76, 84
Emergency Action Plan
    contents 14, 111
    risk control measures 73
    site specific training 60, 61
    toxic gas release 95, 104
    water clarity 69
emergency equipment 69
emergency lighting 82
emergency procedures 67, 71, 77, 103–104
emergency showers 98, 100, 104
emergency vehicle access 38
employees *see* staff
Employers' Liability (Compulsory Insurance) Act 1969 9
employers' responsibilities 6, 15–16
erosion feeders 95
European Standard BSEN 1069:Part 1 28
European Standard EN 60309-2:1998 (formerly BS 4343) 84
European standards, water features 28, 51, 52, 53
*Everyone's guide to RIDDOR* 14
extended life support 58
eyewash facilities 103
face masks 16
fail-safe dosing system 95–96
falling rapids 31, 75
filtration 102–103
FINA 26, 49, 117
finishes
    non-abrasive 21–22
    slip-resistant 21–22, 35, 36, 49
    slippery 42–43
fire hazard 85, 89–90
fire precautions 3, 94
Fire Precautions (Workplace) Regulations 1997 9
fire safety equipment, positioning 40
first aid 15–16, 58, 103–104, 113
*Five steps to risk assessment* 12
floor level changes 22, 35, 76
floors
    cleaning 43
    design 42–43
    finishes 24–25
    gradient 42, 44
    hazards 43, 44
floors *see also* movable floors and bulkheads
food and drink 55, 65, 72, 110
footbaths 35–36
freeboard, high 23, 27, 28, 36, 48
glare and reflection 25, 41, 49, 62, 69
glazing 25, 40–41, 82–83
guard-rails 39
*Guide to the Reporting of Injuries, Diseases and Dangerous Occurrences Regulations 1995* 14–15
hand-rails 21, 24, 35, 46, 50
*Handbook of sports and recreational building design* 25, 81
hazard
    definition 11
    disinfection system 95–97
    most important 55–56
    visibility 35, 36, 37
hazard data sheets 94
hazardous substances 91, 92

health problems see medical conditions
health and safety
    documentation 7
    legal requirements 3, 5
    management 12–13
Health and Safety at Work Etc Act 1974 5–7, 16, 60
Health and Safety (Enforcing Authority) Regulations 1998 9
Health and Safety Executive (HSE) 3, 9, 81, 100, 119–120
Health and Safety (First Aid) Regulations 1981 15–16
Health and Safety (Safety Signs and Signals) Regulations 1996 8, 16, 81, 109
heating, ventilation and air-conditioning 40, 80–81, 82
hoists see pool hoists
hydrogen gas 99
IEE Regulations 40, 84, 86
improper or suspicious behaviour 70
incidents see accidents and incidents
inflatable play structures 75–76
inlets and outlets 21, 44–45, 53
inner-tube rides 30–31, 74
isolation switches 84
learner/training pools 50
legal obligations 3, 5–9
legal requirements 5, 13, 83–84
lifeguards
    accident prevention 56–57
    alertness 57, 62, 64, 80
    attributes and duties 57–59
    clothing 61–62
    employment status 57
    at outdoor facilities 62, 75
    Pool Safety Operating Procedure 59, 60
    provision and deployment 56, 57, 62–64, 71, 73–74
    response 56, 63
    sightlines and access 25, 27, 31, 36, 47, 63, 69
    training 16, 57, 59–61, 113, 114
lighting 82, 83
*Lighting at work* 82
liquified petroleum gas (LPG) 81
local authority, responsibility 3, 9
lockers see storage, lockers
*Maintaining portable and transportable electrical equiment* 86
maintenance 79, 80, 83, 85–87, 96, 100
major injury, definition 15
Management of Health and Safety at Work Regulations 1992 6, 15, 57, 59, 91
*Managing asbestos in workplace buildings* 81
manual handling 68, 93
*Manual handling: Solutions you can handle* 93
*Manual handling. Manual Handling Operations Regulations 1992* 93
Manual Handling Operations Regulations 1989 7–8
manufacturer's instructions 79, 92
manufacturer's responsibilities 6
material safety data sheet (MSDS) 91, 92
medical conditions 55, 77, 110
micro-organisms 90, 97, 103
movable floors and bulkheads 20, 26-29, 30, 49, 76–77
movement joints 24, 43
'must', definition 3
Normal Operating Procedure
    contents 14, 111
    lifeguard numbers 62–63
    preventive maintenance 79
    risk control measures 73
    risk factors 56
    training 57, 60
Notification of Installations Handling Hazardous Substances Regulations 1982 104
NVQs 113
outdoor facilities see pool, natural/open air
oxygen insufflation 16, 58

ozone 101
paddling pools 77
people with disabilities 23, 32, 69, 71, 77, 115–116
personal protective equipment (PPE) 16, 60, 91, 92–93, 98, 101, 103
Personal Protective Equipment Regulations 1992 92
physical barriers 23, 34, 38, 40, 48, 67, 68
planning supervisor 7
pool
    access
        safe 22–24
        unauthorised 68
    construction, demolition or refurbishment 2, 7
    depth see water depth
    design 2, 19
    maximum loading 68
    medical/therapeutic use see spa pools
    natural/open air 2, 68, 75
    private 2
    responsibility for safety 3, 14
    types covered by this guidance 2
pool bottom, design/visibility 20, 21–22, 41
pool covers 37, 68
pool edge 21, 45, 72
pool ends, raised 21, 26, 47, 73
pool hall, temperature 80
pool hire 56, 64, 65, 70, 71, 112
pool hoists 32, 77
pool operator
    chlorine gas precautions 100–101
    and Control of Substances Hazardous to Health (COSHH) Regulations 1994 92
    definition 1
    duty of care 56, 69–70
    and first aid provision 15–16
    legal obligations 5–9
    legal requirements 83–84
    monitoring of water features 75
    and pool hirers 64
    preventive maintenance 79
    responsibilities 1, 2, 7–8, 9, 57, 80, 83–84
    risk assessment 6, 11–12
    risk awareness 55–56
    staff assessments 59
pool owner, responsibilities 1
Pool Safety Operating Procedure
    complying with 59, 60, 61, 64, 65, 71–72
    contents 14, 111
    identifying design problems 33
    paddling pool 77
    revision 61
    specialised equipment 72
    supervision 66, 71
pool surround 23, 34, 35, 45
pool tank, design 20–22, 27, 44–48
pool water see water
Pool Water Treatment Advisory Group 89
Pressure Systems and Transportable Gas Containers Regulations 1989 80
programmed sessions 71
protection of public 80, 93
Provision and Use of Work Equipment Regulations (PUWER) 1998 6–7
public liability insurance 9
pump failure 95
rafts and inflatables 76
ramps 23, 24, 36
'reasonably practicable', definition 2
record keeping 12, 15, 33, 56, 59, 60, 61, 87
Rehabilitation of Offenders Act 1974 70
Reporting of Injuries, Diseases and Dangerous Occurrences Regulations (RIDDOR) 1995 14–15, 60, 67
rescue equipment 67
residual current devices (RCDs) 84–85
respirators 93
resuscitation 16, 58, 61
risk, definition 11

risk assessment
    chemical handling 91, 95
    emergency equipment 69
    glazed areas 83
    inflatable play structures 75–76
    pool operator's responsibility 2, 6, 11–12
    record keeping 12
    safety of people with disabilities 71
    supervision requirements 55
    water clarity 69
    water features 72
risk awareness 55–56
safe working practices 81, 89–90
safety, bathers's responsibility 110
safety features, projecting 46
safety organisations 115
safety policy statement 11–14, 89
safety procedure, written 66
safety signs *see* signs and signals
schools, programmed sessions 71
security measures 67
sightlines 25, 36, 47, 51, 63, 69, 76–77
signs and signals 8, 16–17, 41–42, 56, 71, 77, 109
skin irritation 89, 97
slip-resistant finishes 21–22, 24, 35, 36, 49, 116
slow and fast river rides 31, 75
smoking, prohibition 95, 98
soaker feeders 95
social events 72
sodium bisulphite 102
sodium hypochlorite 94, 98–99
spa pools 2, 31–32, 77
spillage, chemicals 98, 104
spinal injuries 58
Sports Councils 3, 120–121
staff
    positioning 36, 41, 47
    recruitment 69–70
    responsibilies 6, 8
standards, adhering to 3
starting platforms 26, 47, 73
*Step-by-step guide to COSSH assessment* 90
steps and ladders, design 23–24, 46, 50, 51
storage
    chemicals 94, 99, 101
    equipment 32
    fuel 81
    lockers 32, 37, 68
*Storage of LPG at fixed installations* 81
sub-aqua 72, 115
suction hazards 21, 32, 45
supervision
    changing facilities 64, 70
    diving facilities and pools 49, 73
    equipment 72–73
    movable floors and bulkheads 76–77
    programmed sessions 71
    requirements 55, 56, 65, 66
    spa pools 77
    water features 73–75
surface ponding 43
SVQs 113
swimming pool see pool
*Swimming pool water – treatment and quality standards* 45, 93
teachers and coaches 61, 71
temperature, air and water 80
tiles, cracked or broken 45, 72
toxic chemicals 89–90, 93, 104

training
    Control of Substances Hazardous to Health
    (COSHH) Regulations 1994 91–92
    emergency procedures 69
    first aid 113
    lifeguards 16, 57, 59–61, 113, 114
    manual handling 8
    pool hoists 77
    record keeping 59, 60, 61
    spa pools 77
training organisations 114
underwater features, projecting 47
unruly behaviour 34, 56, 67, 73–74, 76, 110
upstands 35–36
ventilation systems see heating, ventilation and air conditioning
violence 67
visibility
    hazards 35, 36, 37
    pool bottom 20, 22, 41
    pool edge 21, 45
    in spa pools 32
    and water clarity 69
    and water features 69
volunteers 5, 6, 57, 62, 65
walls 25, 39–40
warning signs *see* signals and signs
waste disposal 97
water
    chemical monitoring 102
    circulation 95
    clarity 56, 69, 90
    filtration 102–103
    hardness 98
    pH 102
    quality 3, 77, 90
    temperature 81
water depth
    abrupt changes 20, 44
    indicating 20, 22, 29, 41–42, 67
    on initial access 23, 34
    and level of supervision 63
    minimum 20, 70–71
water features
    design 30–31, 48
    European standards 51, 52, 53
    misuse 48
    monitoring by pool operator 75
    risk assessment 72
    usage patterns 35
    and visibility 69
water polo 25, 40
water slides 27, 51–53, 73–74
water surface, visibility 26
water treatment systems 89
wave machines 27, 28, 48, 74
weak swimmers, potentially hazardous 55
wheelchairs 24, 35
Workplace (Health, Safety and Welfare) Regulations 1992 6, 83
    *Appproved Code of Practice* 82, 83
zoning 64

Printed and published by the Health and Safety Executive
**3/99   C150**